D0649318

A **GAME** &
MUCH MORE

Applying Principles of Basketball to the Christian Life

NOEL WHITE

*To: Perry County, Indiana
Bookmobile,
With all good wishes
and gratitude for the time
I lived in Perry County.
Noel White*

DISCARDED

TATE PUBLISHING, LLC

Endorsements

Building on his many years a local church pastor, Noel White reflects on the Christian life through the unique lens of basketball. "A Game and Much More" stretches the imagination by using basketball to illuminate the eternal truths of the Christian faith.
Stephen C. Gray
Conference Minister, Indiana-Kentucky Conference, United Church of Christ

Noel White's early years were spent in southeastern Kentucky. Whatever his parents instilled in him, the boys of the small town of Barbourville wanted. Most of the eyes that were on young Noel were boys that wanted to be able to run track and play basketball like he did. Basketball is king in Kentucky and anyone who has ever put a hoop up on a barn or gone to the sawmill to get boards for a backboard or dreamed of shooting the game winning shot will enjoy reading about Noel's motivation. Noel brilliantly and successful captures the secret gift that faith plays in all the games young people play.
Bert Scent
Photo Editor, Barbourville Mountain Advocate

After having been responsible for the nation's largest high school state tournament (the Kentucky Sweet Sixteen) for many years, I know first hand the passion that people from the Commonwealth have for basketball. Noel White has captured the essence of that enthusiasm, linking it to life lessons and fundamentals of the Christian life which are necessary for strong character foundation that will last a lifetime.
Julian Tackett
Associate Commissioner of the Kentucky High School Athletic Association

DEDICATION

To Nevil White, a pastor, my father, anchor, role model and encourager; And

To Herman Bush, my college basketball coach, and mentor, who enabled me to believe in myself, for which I am eternally grateful.

They gave me more than I can ever repay, but through this book, I hope to share some of their values.

Acknowledgement

Appreciation is expressed to:

Betty Jane, my wife, without whose love, patience, encouragement, and secretarial skills, this book would not have been possible;

John Noel and Mary Jane, our adult children, whose interest, suggestions and support are not only a part of this book, but a part of our lives;

The many people in the communities where we have lived and the churches where we have served who have encouraged Betty Jane and me, inspiring us to share with others the ideas found in this book;

And to the staff at Tate Publishing who saw the validity of these concepts and shared many supportive ideas.

TABLE OF CONTENTS

Introduction

"Why don't you go home and get some religion from your father? Then you might be able to play basketball." This is what my high school coach said to me in the dressing room, in front of my teammates, after a district tournament game. I know he was trying to motivate me, but I didn't understand the analogy of religion and playing basketball. He may have known, although he never mentioned it, that James Naismith, the inventor of basketball, was also an ordained minister, a fact that must have had an influence on the ideas in his game.

Whether that incident planted the seed that eventually grew into this book, I am not certain. I am sure, however, that from childhood to the present day, Christianity and basketball have been important parts of my life. Growing up and living in Kentucky, where basketball is almost a religion, has contributed to this fascination.

In college, my basketball coach gave me the gift of self-confidence and enabled me to believe in myself. I realized that Christ had done this for His followers, and I dreamed of being a coach that would enable players to have confidence in basketball and in life. After graduating from college, with a major in physical education, I went to graduate school, fully intending to become a coach. While there, I felt God's call to pastoral ministry.

During my years of ministry, whether writing sermons, working with groups, or in personal counseling, I found myself constantly using basketball analogies. I shared concepts like following God as coach, working together as a team, rebounding a missed shot, letting go of mistakes and the significance of each participant.

I also emphasized the importance of small groups, each one of which had about the same number of participants as a basketball team. We even changed the names of committees to teams.

Jesus' use of illustrative analogies has always fascinated me. I believe that if He was living in the 21st century, because basketball is such a popular sport, He would use an analogy such as "the Christian life is like basketball," and then he would refer to a specific aspect of the game. He would use this technique to enable his listeners to better understand his teachings. This book uses that format.

The purpose of this book is to relate the Christian life to basketball, and to share a practical, easily understood faith which relates to daily life. My hope is that the reader will come to understand the Christian life in a new way and to appreciate that God is concerned about every aspect of life - from our dirty, smelly feet to our eternal home with Him.

Noel White

CHOOSING UP SIDES

Did you ever get upset when it came time to choose sides for a basketball game and they didn't choose you? Or, maybe they chose you, but it was reluctantly. Of course, the gist of these scenarios is that choosing the strongest team members gives the team its best chance to win.

Kenneth E. Jones

The thrill of being chosen to participate on a team brings with it a strong sense of belonging and purpose.

In the small town where I grew up, there weren't a lot of organized athletic activities which required parents to run a schedule and drive us from one place to another. But that didn't stop us from playing basketball. We knew where all the goals were in town, and every day we would be there shooting baskets. Soon someone would say, "Let's choose up sides and play a game." You always felt important and appreciated when you were one of the first to be chosen. Not to be chosen, however, was painful and embarrassing.

When I was in the seventh grade I went out for the junior varsity basketball team. I can still remember the hurt and humiliation I felt when I was not chosen to be on the team. In the eleventh grade I played on the varsity team. Even though I lettered, I was not chosen to be on the team for the district and regional tournaments. No explanation was given and I felt betrayed and rejected. The following week the head coach of the neighboring high school shared with me that he had told my coach how surprised he was that I was not on the tournament team. He said he would have chosen me because he thought I was our team's best middle man on the fast break. I remember thinking to myself, "If I could, I would choose to play for that coach."

Many people consider Michael Jordan to be the best all-around basketball player who ever lived. As a sophomore in high school, however, he was not chosen to play on his school's basketball team. He was told he was not good enough. He went home, went to his room and cried uncontrollably. As a result of that experience, however, he began to work harder on his game. That work ethic continued through his pro career. It is rare for an athlete, who has been cut from his high school team, to reach the professional level. Michael Jordan's painful disappointment at not being chosen to play on the team was so strong that he never wanted to have that feeling again, so he worked hard on his game throughout his career.

Why is it so important to be chosen to play on a basketball team? It is an awesome privilege and a tremendous experience. The benefits include working together with teammates to accomplish goals, challenging each person to play his best, and supporting each other and the team in facing the demands of the season. With each passing game, a team chemistry develops, forming friendships and making individuals stronger. The basketball team represents the school or institution for which they play, as a type of advertisement. They know that supporting them are teachers, administrators, students, and parents who count on them to be positive emissaries in their sportsmanship and in the way they play the game. Being chosen to play on a team can be one of life's greatest experiences. But an even greater blessing is the opportunity to be on Christ's team.

Can you imagine how fulfilled and grateful you would be if Christ saw something in you that would prompt Him to choose you to join His team? The good news is that this has already happened. He said, "It is not that you have chosen me, but that I have chosen you."[1]

Being chosen to share in the team fellowship of Christ and His followers is similar to being on a basketball team, but is an even greater experience. There is the joy of living in the love and guidance of Christ. He promised this when He said, "I have told you this so that you can share my joy, and your joy may be complete."[2] Even though we are all unique in the camaraderie of the Christian community, lasting relationships are developed. Christ expressed this when He said, "This is my commandment: that you love each other as I have loved you. There is no greater love than this: that a man should lay down his life for his friends."[3] We are also representatives of Christ when we are in the fellowship of His team. He said, "I have appointed you to go and bear fruit."[4] The way to bear fruit and be good representatives of the Christian way is to show the new purpose in life that Christ provides. Our purpose is not to confront or threaten, but to be positive advertisements, attracting others to the fellowship.

The good news is that Christ has chosen us. The challenge is that we must decide if we choose to accept the life He offers. Jesus told a very touching story about a young man who chose not to accept the life his father had given him.

"There was once a man who had two sons. The younger said to his father, 'Father, I want right now what's coming to me.'

"So the father divided the property between them. It wasn't long before the younger son packed his bags and left for a distant country. There, undisciplined and dissipated, he wasted everything he had. After he had gone through all his money, there was a bad famine all through that country and he began to hurt. He signed on with a citizen there who assigned him to his fields to slop the pigs. He was so hungry he would have eaten the corncobs in the pig slop, but no one would give him any.

"That brought him to his senses. He said, 'All those farmhands working for my father sit down to three meals a day, and here I am starving to death.

I'm going back to my father. I'll say to him, "Father, I've sinned against God, I've sinned before you; I don't deserve to be called your son ever again."'

"When he was still a long way off, his father saw him. His heart pounding, he ran out, embraced him, and kissed him. The son started his speech: 'Father, I've sinned against God, I've sinned before you. I don't deserve to be called your son ever again.'

"But the father wasn't listening. He was calling to the servants, 'Quick.Bring a clean set of clothes and dress him. Put the family ring on his finger and sandals on his feet. Then get a grain-fed heifer and roast it. We're going to feast! We're going to have a wonderful time! My son is here—given up for dead and now alive! Given up for lost and now found!' And they began to have a wonderful time."[5]

What an amazing story! The son chose to leave his father and realized he had made a terrible mess of his life. When he chose to go back home, he was amazed to see his father running down the road to meet him. He was even more flabbergasted when his father joyfully chose to welcome him back and throw a huge celebration. Wow! Jesus said that God is like that father. He always chooses us first, but before the transaction is complete, we must choose God in return.

There are many things in life we cannot choose. We cannot choose our birthplace, our race, our parents, our siblings, our gender, or our height. But we can choose whether we want to accept our Lord's choice of us.

When Jesus was dying on the cross, there were two thieves hanging beside Him. One thief chose to mock and ridicule Him. The other, however, chose to ask Jesus to remember him when He entered His kingdom. To that thief, Jesus said, "Today, you shall be with me in paradise."[6] That thief had made many bad choices in his life, but they were all cancelled when he made the choice to ask Jesus to let him be a part of His kingdom.

You see, the transaction of being chosen is not complete until we decide to choose back. This was illustrated in an episode of "Gunsmoke," the long-running Western television show. Festus was a deputy sheriff who had a cousin named Billy Hagen, often called Sweet Billy Hagen. Sweet Billy came down out of the mountains to choose a wife. He chose Miss Kitty, who ran the Long Branch Saloon. The trouble was that Miss Kitty didn't like Sweet Billy that much - partly the smell, largely the looks. He was the ugliest, bad-smelling person you ever saw. You could almost smell him through the television.

Sweet Billy walks into the Long Branch Saloon one night to tell Miss Kitty that he has chosen her to be his wife. Miss Kitty tells Billy that she is too busy running the Long Branch Saloon, and she does not want to go up to his cabin to do his laundry and cook his meals. She suggests, "Billy, why don't you just be a nice boy, have a beer and leave?" After several beers, Sweet Billy decides that he is going to leave, but he is going to take Miss Kitty with him. His Paw had told him to go to town and choose a wife, and Miss Kitty is who he chose.

So after drinking his beer, he makes his way up the back stairway and hides out in Miss Kitty's apartment. About one o'clock she comes home from work. As she comes through the door, Sweet Billy grabs her, gags her, ties her up and throws her in his wagon. He is going to carry her up the mountain to be his wife. Miss Kitty's not very happy about that. She's thinking nasty words all the way up the hill.

After Sweet Billy gets her to his cabin, Miss Kitty is so hostile that he has to chain her to the front porch post, "till she should fall in love of me," as he said. One day Sweet Billy's Paw comes over to the house to counsel with him in this difficult period of his life. The conversation goes something like this:

Paw: "She don't seem to be comin' around, does she son?"

Sweet Billy: "No, Paw, she don't."

Paw: What do you think might be the problem, son?"

Sweet Billy: "I don't know, Paw. I chose her, but she won't choose me back. I chose her but she won't choose me back."

You see, it's the choosing back that is so important. Christ has chosen us, but we must choose him back. In the story that Jesus told of the son that left home, it would have been one thing for the father to stand on the porch and say, "Where could my son be?" But it is another thing for the son to choose to go back home. Yes, the father could have gone out and dragged the son back and chained him to the porch post, but that is not the same thing as the boy choosing to come home to his father. More than that, when he comes home, he now realizes how chosen he is by the father.

It is a tremendous thing to be chosen to play on a basketball team. That pales in comparison, however, to the benefits we receive from God choosing us to be on His team. And we have been chosen.

The Scripture says, "But you are the ones chosen by God, chosen for the high calling of priestly work, chosen to be a holy people, God's instruments to do His work and speak out for Him, to tell others of the night-and-day difference He made for you—from nothing to something, from rejected to accepted."[7]

Good news! God has chosen us. Will we choose Him back? Will we choose to be on His team?

Point Guard

The point guard is the coach on the floor; his role is to start the offensive wheels turning. He should be the most level-headed player on the court, if not the one who's most respected by his teammates.

Richard "Digger" Phelps

In the book *My Losing Season,* best selling author Pat Conroy describes a big change that began to take place in basketball when the concept of point guard was introduced to the game. Until that time most coaches would put five players on the floor who were their best scorers. Generally there was not a skilled passer among them. Innovators of the game were beginning to see the importance of having a guard whose primary responsibility was to distribute the ball to the big men.[8]

Pat Conroy writes that his team, The Citadel, was playing Auburn, a strong team from the Southeastern Conference. As he watched from the bench, Pat studied the play of Auburn's point guard, Bobby Buisson, determined to learn as much as he could and adapt his own talents to that position. He observed how much Buisson wanted to be there for his teammates, the joy he had in delivering a pass to an open player, and the gratitude Buisson's teammates felt in being recipients of his distribution skills.[9] Later, as the season progressed, Pat Conroy learned that in order to be a successful point guard, he had to distribute the ball as evenly as possible to his teammates, making sure each player got his fair share of the shots.

The concept of point guard revolutionized

basketball, adding to the excitement and making it more of a team game. The leading scorers know they are going to get their shots because a teammate, generally the point guard, will pass them the ball.

In life, as well as in basketball, every person needs someone to pass them the ball if they are going to be successful. That person may be a teenager who feels lonely and insecure - and a word of positive affirmation or some quality time is passed to them, giving them encouragement. It may be an older person, close to retirement, who wonders if anything of value has been accomplished during his working years - when a statement of appreciation for his faithfulness and influence is passed to him, giving his life meaning. That person may be a pastor, serving a challenging congregation, wondering if anyone cares about the prayerful effort being made - and anonymous postcards of support, signed by "mc," are mailed to him, giving him motivation. (Only years later does he learn that "mc" stands for "member of congregation"). It may be a family member, spouse or child, who feels unloved - when an affirmative word of love is expressed and personal time is shared, lifting his or her spirit.

In the Biblical book of Genesis, chapter eleven, there is the story of people wanting to make a name for themselves by building a tower that will reach to the heavens. The Lord is not pleased with their selfish motivation and stops the construction of the tower by confusing their language. (Until that time, all people spoke the same language.) This is why the structure is called the Tower of Babel. This Biblical story inspired Noah Ben Shea to write in his book, *Jacob's Journey,* "The difference between a Tower of Babel and a tower of strength is the difference between those who live to make themselves more and those who know the way to heaven is making others more."[10] The joy of making others more, of passing the ball to them, is the point guard mentality.

Toward the end of the book *My Losing Season,* Pat Conroy writes:

> "I turned myself into the best point guard I was capable of being. That I averaged twelve points a game, and scored over twenty points in four college games that season, dazzles my imagination even now and reinforces the fact that belief in oneself—authentic, inviolable, and unshakable belief, not the undercutting kind—is necessary to all human achievement. Once I began believing in myself and not listening to the people who did not believe in me, I turned myself into a point guard who you needed to watch. I could bring it up court. I could stick it in your face. I could take care of the ball. I could get it to the big men and I could work the break. By the end of the season, I came at the whole world like a point guard. Point guard. It's the most beautiful phrase in sports to me."[11]

Believing in yourself and in the person to whom the ball is being passed is essential for a point guard mentality in basketball and in life. Maybe you have never heard the name of William Marcy, although the highest mountain in New York State is named for him. Several generations ago, Bill Marcy was a wild young ruffian in Southbridge, Massachusetts, who led a gang of boys who literally drove their high school teacher out of town and dared him to return. The school board finally called another teacher, a man whose name was Salem Town, and everybody watched to see who would win the contest of intellect and brawn.

Now shift the scene and skip several years. Bill Marcy is the guest of honor at a dinner given by the governor. Suddenly Mr. Marcy leaves the head table, to go out into the crowd where he embraces an old man - a teacher by the name of Salem Town. "Do you two know each other?" asked the Governor. "Do I know him?" said

Marcy. "This is the man who made me. When I was a boy, no one, not even my father, saw any good in me. He was the first person who ever believed in me. I owe more to him than to any living person." William Marcy was a U. S. Senator, three times the governor of the State of New York, and was Secretary of State in the President's cabinet. In his time of need as a boy, somebody believed in him, believed in the possibilities of his personality and threw him the ball.

Jesus had a point guard mentality and he used it often. He used it when a woman was brought to him who had been caught in the act of adultery; he used it with the woman at the well in Samaria; and he used it with Zaccheus, the tax collector. He used it with the group of smelly, loud fishermen and peasants whom he chose for his disciples. His point guard mentality was seen as He brought out each person's finest possibilities, passing them the ball and letting them know He believed in them.

Somebody needs you or me in exactly this fashion. They need us to show them that we believe in the possibilities of their personalities by passing them the ball of affirmation. When that happens, all are better for it. As Andrew Carnegie said, "It marks a big step in your development to realize that other people can help you do a better job than you could do alone."[12]

Have you ever thought that God has a "point guard" mentality, passing the ball to us because He believes in us? For example, He has entrusted us with the strength to lift an arm. He knows that, having this power, we can reach out and bless people or we can close our fist and beat them into the dust. When God passes such power to us, He is taking a terrific chance. Surely He must believe in us, trusting that we will use the power He passes to us to make life better for everyone.

If you want to see how much God really believes in us, look at the Cross where He allowed His Son to die for our sins. As we watch Jesus suffer we find ourselves asking, "Does God believe there is something valuable in me that He would allow His Son's death to take place for me? He knows how weak I am. Can He possibly believe in me that much?"

Yes, God does believe in us that much, and with His point guard mentality He passes the ball of forgiveness and eternal life to us. Because He has done that, He expects us to score by passing to the people around us affirmation, hope, support, and love.

Pat Conroy could very well be right. "Point guard" is the most beautiful phrase in sports, and in life.

Way Up When You're Down

When you've made big mistakes and your life appears to be headed for shipwreck, who can help? Are there any promises more comforting than God's? When you feel anxious today, STOP. Pray: "God, I trust in your faithfulness to change both my attitude and my circumstances."

The Devotional Bible

Faith is an attitude of hope about the future - a belief that there is a way up when we're down. Basketball and the Christian life have been channels of hope and a way up for numerous people who have been in the depths of life.

One such person is Allen Iverson. Born in the projects of Hampton, Virginia, when his mother was fifteen years of age, his father was never present for support. His grandmother, the pillar of the family, died soon after he was born. Allen's mother, Ann, had difficulty paying the bills, so there were many days of no electricity, no heat, no water, and no food. But Ann never stopped reassuring Allen, telling him he could become whatever he wanted to be. She encouraged him to become involved in athletics, something that became a form of release for him from the struggles at home. He was very competitive and ultimately led his high school to state championships in football and basketball. In his senior year he was involved in a fight and was sentenced to five years in jail for throwing a chair at a girl. Doug Wilder, governor of Virginia, seeing potential in Allen, granted him conditional release, but his future still seemed uncertain. Eventually, John Thompson, the legendary tough-love coach at Georgetown University, recruited him to play basketball. Finally, Allen had a father figure in Coach Thompson, under whose guidance he thrived. In his sophomore year he was named an All-American. Because he needed money to help support his mother and sister, Iverson declared himself for the professional draft. He was the first player drafted, fulfilling the dream his mother had placed in his heart - that he could be whatever he wanted to be.

As a professional, Iverson has been somewhat controversial because of his candidness and heavily tattooed body, but he is one of the NBA's leading scorers. In 2004 he represented the United States on the Olympic basketball team, because of his conviction that it was important to play for his country and to keep a commitment he had made two years earlier. He was unanimously elected co-captain by his teammates. Iverson, who is very loyal to his family and the people he knew before achieving stardom, has used basketball as a way to make his way up when he was down.[13]

A basketball player with a similar story is LaBron James. There seemed to be little hope for him early in his life. He and his mother, Gloria, moved from apartment to apartment in Akron, Ohio. In the fourth grade, because of little parental discipline, he missed more than eighty days of school. His mother allowed him to move in and live with the family of his peewee football coach, Frankie Walker. James says that this experience turned his life around. He didn't miss a single day of class in the fifth grade. He calls his perfect-attendance certificate the most important award he has received. Walker's wife, Pam, helped Gloria find a permanent apartment for herself and LeBron. With his life more settled, he eventually became the best high school basketball player in the country and went professional after graduation. At the age of twenty he became the youngest player to reach one of the toughest performance milestones in basketball, the "triple double" (double digits in points, rebounds, and assists in a single game,) and he did it again three nights later. A versatile performer, he is considered by many to be the best player in the National Basketball Association today.[14]

The stories of Allen Iverson and LaBron James are quite unique. Many teenagers who live in poverty dream of playing professional basketball, but only a microscopic fraction of thousands ever make it. Basketball does provide for many of them, however, the chance to receive an education at a college or university through an athletic scholarship. It's a channel of hope, providing a way up when they're down.

For many young people who are trapped in the slums or the inner city, playground basketball is a way of life. In numerous cities, basketball camps provide activities that involve more than just play. In addition to drills, shooting exercises, and individual coaching, the youth learn values, how to play aggressively without fighting, and the danger of drugs. Community leaders know the importance of organized sports in an economically poor neighborhood. Not only do sports provide entertainment and distraction, they encourage discipline and focus, skills that are keys to finding and keeping jobs.

Trevor Williams leads a basketball camp in Montreal, the same camp he attended as a youth. After going to Southern University in Baton Rouge, Louisiana, on a basketball scholarship, in 1992 he played for Team Canada in the Barcelona Olympics. Williams says that it was through basketball that he learned such key life skills as anger management, conflict resolution, discipline, tolerance, and the importance of helping others. Through the basketball camp he passes those same values to the next generation. The players think they are learning basketball, but that's only the carrot to get them to the camp. What they are being taught is the game of life that provides them with a channel of hope for the future.

Tony Campolo, professor emeritus of sociology at Eastern University in St. David's, Pennsylvania, told how he used basketball as a channel of hope.

"I was working in Philadelphia. We had seven summer camps in urban neighborhoods with disadvantaged, at-risk kids. In each of the camps we had a basketball team. At the end of the season, I got an all-star team together from all of those respective neighborhoods, and we staged a basketball game against the Philadelphia Eagles Football Team. It was a good public relations event that I staged at Eastern University where I teach. I had the kids in the dressing room of Eastern University, and we were all getting jacked up to go out and play this game against the Philadelphia Eagles. The kids couldn't believe it. These were the stars they had seen on television, and they were going to get to play against them. I said to these kids, 'I brought you out here to the college because I want you to imagine yourselves playing on this basketball court someday and with God's help, you can do it."

" The man who had been chosen to coach the all-stars interrupted me and said, 'Don't listen to this man. Don't listen to this man! People like that have told me I could escape from the ghetto, that I could make something of myself. I tried,' he said to those kids. 'I really tried and look at me. I'm right back where I started from. So don't let him put fancy dreams into your head. Do you understand? Don't let him put fancy visions in your skull.

" Campolo hardly knew what to say and then a poem by Shel Silverstein came to him. He modified it just a bit. He said to those African-American kids, who he could see were shocked by their coach,

      'Listen to the mustn'ts, child.
      Listen to the don'ts.
      Listen to the never could bes.
      Listen to the won'ts.
      Listen to the never have beens.
      Then listen close to me.
      Anything can happen, child.
      Anything can be.'
'Now let's go out and play ball.' And they did."[15]

That's the hope that basketball can bring and that's the hope of the Christian life. Jesus says, "I have a way up for you when you're down. I have a future for you. I don't care where you are or what condition you're in, you're here on this planet because there are good things for you to do. There are great things for you to be."

It is God's business to bring people up when they're down. The Psalmist was aware of this when he wrote:

"Hear my cry, O God; listen to my prayer. From the ends of the earth I call to you, I call as my heart grows faint; lead me to the rock that is higher than I."[16]

The hymn writer fully understood that God is in the business of lifting people up when he wrote:

      "I'm pressing on the upward way,
      new heights I'm gaining every day;
      Still praying as I'm onward bound,
'Lord, plant my feet on higher ground.' My heart has no desire to stay where doubts arise and fears dismay;
      Though some may dwell where these abound,
My prayer, my aim is higher ground. Lord, lift me up and let me stand by faith on heaven's tableland.
A higher plane than I have found: Lord, plant my feet on higher ground."[17]

God has a purpose for lifting us up which is to make something beautiful out of our lives even though we may seem as hopeless as a blob of clay. This is the analogy the prophet Jeremiah uses to describe the amazing way God works with us.

"This is the word the Lord spoke to Jeremiah: 'Go down to the potter's house, and I will give you my message there.' So I went down to the potter's house and saw him working at the potter's wheel. He was using his hands to make a pot from clay, but something went wrong with it. So he used that clay to make another pot the way he wanted it to be.

"Then the Lord spoke His word to me: 'Family of Israel, can't I do the same thing with you?' says the Lord. 'You are in my hands like the clay in the potter's hands.'"[18]

From this Scripture comes the Gospel song:

"Have Thine own way, Lord! Have Thine own way!

Thou art the Potter, I am the clay.

Mold me and make me after Thy will,

While I am waiting, yielded and still." [19]

Seventy years later Bill and Gloria Gaither wrote a chorus that expresses the same conviction:

"Something beautiful, something good;

All my confusion He understood;

All I had to offer Him was brokenness and strife,

But He made something beautiful of my life."[20]

That's the reason God sent His Son into the world - to make something beautiful out of us when we're broken, to show us the way up when we're down, and to give us hope for the future. This action gift of God is available to all people, no matter how low they have sunk or how sinful they have been.

These words of Phillip Yancey are a challenge to every person, particularly those who have already been lifted up by God:

"Somehow we have created a community of respectability in the church. The down-and-out, who flocked to Jesus when he lived on earth, no longer feel welcome. How did Jesus, the only perfect person in history, manage to attract the notoriously imperfect? And what keeps us from following in His steps today?"[21]

Every person must remember that Christians are not people who are illustrations of goodness. They are people who are down, or have been down, and through Christ are experiencing a way up. And so the Christian community is a place where people are lifted up, are made beautiful through the active love of God, and experience a brand new life.

Basketball and the Christian life continue to be channels of hope for those who are down and need a way up.

DIRTY, SMELLY FEET

Your most important pieces of sports equipment, your feet, are a complex system of muscles, bones, and ligaments that act as springs, levers, pivots, and launching pads.

Peter Weiss

Dirty, smelly feet - not the most refined parts of the body, but a real priority in basketball and in Jesus' life.

Many people consider John Wooden to be the greatest coach in the history of college basketball. His UCLA teams won ten national championships, including seven in a row (1966–1973.) Six times he was voted the NCAA Coach of the Year. He is one of two people enshrined in the Basketball Hall of Fame as both a player and a coach.

With such outstanding achievements, it seems amazing that one of the first things Coach Wooden taught his players was how to care for their feet. It was his firm conviction that a player could be no better than his feet allowed him to be. If a player's feet hurt, if his shoes didn't fit, or if he had blisters, he could not play the game at his best. So Coach Wooden taught his players, step-by-step, how to put on a pair of socks properly, so the socks would not wrinkle and cause blisters. He showed his new recruits, step by painstaking step, how to knot their shoelaces so they would never, ever come undone during a game. He also made sure that each player was fitted with the right sized shoe. The toe of the foot was to be at the end of the shoe when the player was standing still, so the foot would not slide forward when a quick stop was to be made.

Today, choosing an athletic shoe is very complicated. Not too long ago, people purchased what they called tennis shoes or sneakers. These shoes weren't for sneaking around, and maybe they weren't even for playing tennis, but they were all pretty much the same—cloth shoes that laced up and produced dirty, smelly feet. Acquiring athletic shoes today is very involved, because it is necessary to choose between walking shoes, tennis shoes, basketball shoes, cross training shoes and so forth. In addition, there are options between leather and cloth, high tops or low. Wow! We go through all of this because of concern for the care of our feet.

When Jesus walked the earth, He confronted a myriad of challenges and struggles. Isn't it amazing, therefore, that when He was facing the most difficult time of His life, He was concerned about His disciples' feet? Persons who know they have a short time to live generally try to achieve what they feel is most important. When Jesus was facing His death, one of the final things He wanted to do was to share a meal with His disciples. It was at that meal that Jesus told His followers there were two things He wanted them to do to remember Him. First, they should share a meal together and call it the Lord's Supper. Most of His followers have done very well at that, regularly celebrating that sacramental meal. The second thing He told His followers they should do was to wash one another's feet.[22] Washing feet is a lowly, smelly, unappreciated task, but Jesus is asking His followers to humble themselves and serve in ways that are uncalled for or unexpected. We could do much better with that directive from our Lord.

Perhaps pastors and religious leaders set the tone for this. When they lead a worship service or speak in a religious setting, they wear long robes, expensive silk stoles and sometimes, academic hoods. It gives an erudite and even superior appearance. Jesus would not have worn that paraphernalia. The only thing He owned was a seamless robe. Wouldn't it be more appropriate for religious leaders, who want to emphasize that they are followers of Jesus, to wear towels around their shoulders in public worship services, symbolizing humility and servanthood?

Jesus clearly revealed his priority during the last meal with His disciples.[23] They were eating together when an argument developed concerning which disciples would be the greatest. What a disappointment their bickering must have been to Jesus, but He didn't express His feelings in words. Instead, He got up from the meal, put a towel over His shoulder, took a pitcher, poured water in a basin, knelt before the disciples and began to wash their feet.

Jesus Christ, the Son of God, behaving as a servant, on His hands and knees, washing and drying each disciple's grimy, dirty feet. He knew about each one of them: James and John, who wanted special treatment and honor; Philip, who on one occasion doubted there was enough food to feed a large crowd; Thomas, who seemed to doubt everything; Peter, who would deny he knew the Lord; Judas, who would betray Him. He knew about all of their transgressions. Not one disciple was worthy for Jesus to relate to him as a servant. But Jesus didn't wash their feet as a nice gesture, or to stop their bickering. He did it because it was necessary. In fact he said, "If I don't wash your feet, you are not one of my people."[24]
Max Lucado writes:

"Jesus did not say, 'If *you* don't wash *your* feet.' Why not? Because we cannot. We cannot cleanse our own filth. We cannot remove our own sin.

Our feet must be in His hands.

"Don't miss the meaning here. To place our feet in the basin of Jesus is to place the filthiest parts of our lives into His hands. In the ancient

East, people's feet were caked with mud and dirt. The servant of the feast saw to it that the feet were cleaned. Jesus is assuming the role of the servant. He will wash the grimiest part of our life. If we let Him. The water of the Servant comes only when we confess that we are dirty. Only when we confess that we are caked with filth, that we have walked forbidden trails and followed the wrong paths."[25]

Has anyone ever washed your feet in a public setting? It happened to me on a hot August day at Lake Junaluska, North Carolina. I had been camping in a tent while attending a week-long workshop on Christian education. As the week progressed, I developed a friendship with one of the men in the group. The last day of the workshop, each person was given the assignment of demonstrating how to communicate without using verbal language, without using words. Each person took their turn. At the appropriate time, my new friend carried a paper bag over to where I was sitting. He knelt before me and gave me some grapes, along with a cracker, symbolizing the Lord's Supper. Then he removed my tennis shoes and socks, took a jar of water from his paper bag, poured it out, and began to wash my feet. Now my feet had been in tennis shoes that had more than permanent foot odor. I had worn the same shoes and socks throughout the entire hot, dusty week. But he never grimaced or held his nose. Then he dried my feet and put on my shoes and socks, never saying a word. It was an experience I have never forgotten. I was so dirty - even smelly - but I felt fresh newness, unconditional acceptance and deep love.

Jesus Christ, the Savior, came as a servant. He told His followers that each one is to find ways to serve by bringing newness to others, accepting them unconditionally, and sharing with people the gift of love. In fact He commanded us "to love one another, as I have loved you."[26]

"Feet!
    Just plain
    ordinary,
    tired
    feet!
He didn't ignore
    the head,
    the heart,
    the soul
    —-spectacular things like that.
But I'm especially glad
    that He cared
    about feet.
Not many messiahs
    ever did that.
You can wax eloquent
    and be beautifully abstract
    about people's
    heads, and hearts, and souls.
But it's hard to be
    removed from human need
    when you're kneeling down on the floor
    washing another person's
    feet.
Dusty roads are scarce
    and very few sandals are worn
    these days,
    but feet trapped in leather
    are just as tired
    —-and just as ignored.
There still aren't
    many messiahs around
    who care about
    feet."[27]

Dirty, smelly feet. A real priority in basketball and in the Christian life.

The Community of a Team

The community of a team is so close that you have to talk with one another; the travel is so constant that you have to interact with one another; the competition is so intense that you have to challenge one another; the game is so fluid that you have to depend on one another; the high and low moments are so frequent that you learn to share them; the season is so long that it brings you to mutual acceptance.

Bill Bradley

The most important measure of how good a game I played was how much better I'd made my teammates play.

Bill Russell

The experience of community on a basketball team or in life enables an individual to become much more than he could ever become alone. It is an unwritten law of human nature that people flourish best when they are working together to achieve something bigger than individual ambition. Retired or injured athletes, no longer able to participate, say that, most of all, they miss the feeling of community and the effort shared with teammates as they strive for a cause bigger than any individual could accomplish alone.

In the Bible, the writer of Ecclesiastes states, "Two are better than one, because they have a good return for their work. If one falls down, his friend can help him up. Also, if two lie down together, they will keep warm. But how can one keep warm alone? Though one may be overpowered, two can defend themselves. A cord of three strands is not quickly broken."[28]

This Scripture is saying that when people work together as a team many positive things happen: they have a good return for their work, they help each other up when they are down, each person is given the warmth of encouragement, and individuals are made stronger than they would ever be alone. In other words, when a team works in community, each individual is made stronger. Michael Jordan, who is considered by many to be the best individual basketball player of all time, wrote in his book, *I Can't Accept Not Trying,*

"There are plenty of teams in every sport that have great players and never win titles. Most of the time, those players aren't willing to sacrifice for the greater good of the team. The funny thing is, in the end, their unwillingness to sacrifice only makes individual goals more difficult to achieve. One thing I believe to the fullest is that if you think and achicvc as a tcam, the individual accolades will take care of themselves. Talent wins games, but teamwork and intelligence win championships."

When John Wooden was coach at UCLA, he made it clear that if you wanted to play for him, team ball was a requirement. In his recruiting, through observation, recommendations, and interviews with coaches of opposing teams, he was determined to see if an athlete had the psychological make-up to play with a group. Sometimes a player, who did not buy into the team concept, hoped that his quickness and athleticism would be so extraordinary that Coach Wooden would feel it was imperative to play him. Without exception, that person would find himself sitting on the bench until he learned that the only way to get playing time was to fit in with the group.[29]

Coach Wooden sold his players on the fabulous

possibilities that were attainable through team effort. Bill Walton described this beautifully when he said,

> "He challenged us to believe that something special could come from the group effort. We live in a society that is constantly pushing us to be individual, to be selfish. But Coach Wooden constantly focused on the group, and how there could be no success unless everybody believed in the same goal and everybody came out of there feeling good about the success of others."[30]

The importance of teamwork can be seen in every area of life. Coach John Wooden often used the analogy of a powerful car to help his players understand this basic concept. There may be a star on the team, which is like a big engine in the car, but if one tire is flat, the car is going nowhere. And if there are brand new tires, but the lug nuts are missing, the wheels come off. Obviously, the powerful engine is no good now. A lug nut may not seem important, but it must be present and properly installed, if the car is going to move. The application is obvious. There is an important role for each team member to play. A person may aspire to what he feels is a larger or more important role, but first the role that has been assigned must be fulfilled. The little things make the big things happen. The big engine cannot make the car move unless the little things are done properly.[31]

The importance of teamwork can be seen in family life. One of the priceless episodes on TV's "The Andy Griffith Show" occurred in the early life of the series. Following the death of his wife, Sheriff Andy Taylor decided to invite his spinster Aunt Bee to come and live with Opie and him, thinking that she would add a missing feminine touch. Surprisingly, Opie was not pleased for Aunt Bee to come in and try to "replace" his mother. Andy tried to help the situation by inviting Aunt Bee to go fishing and frog-catching with them so Opie could become attached to her. Instead, she failed miserably at fishing, frogging and later football. Finally, late one night, after Opie was in bed, Aunt Bee talked with Andy about taking her to the bus station. Opie heard her crying beneath his bedroom window and guessed she was leaving. He ran down the stairs and explained, "We can't let her go, Pa, she needs us. She can't even catch frogs, or take fish off the hook or throw a football. We've got to take care of her or she'll never make it."

We all need each other and this is strikingly true in the Christian life. In the Bible, Paul uses the analogy of the human body to illustrate the importance of each part.

"A person's body is only one thing, but it has many parts. Though there are many parts to a body, all those parts make only one body. Christ is like that also. Some of us are Jews, and some are Greeks. Some of us are slaves, and some are free. But we were all baptized into one body through one Spirit. And we were all made to share in the one Spirit.

"The human body has many parts. The foot might say, 'Because I am not a hand, I am not part of the body.' But saying this would not stop the foot from being a part of the body. The ear might say, 'Because I am not an eye, I am not part of the body.' But saying this would not stop the ear from being a part of the body. If the whole body were an eye, it would not be able to hear. If the whole body were an ear, it would not be able to smell. If each part of the body were the same part, there would be no body. But truly God put all the parts, each one of them, in the body as He wanted them. So then there are many parts, but only one body.

"The eye cannot say to the hand, 'I don't need you!' And the head cannot say to the foot, 'I don't need you.' No! Those parts of the body that seem to be the weaker are really necessary. And the parts of the body we think are less deserving are parts to which we give the most honor. We give special respect to the parts we want to hide. The more respectable parts of our body need no special care. But God put the body together and gave more honor to the parts that need it so our body would not be divided. God wanted the different parts to care the same for each other. If one part of the body suffers, all the other parts suffer with it. Or if one part of our body is honored, all the other parts share its honor.

"Together you are the body of Christ, and each one of you is part of that body."[32]

What a wonderful description Paul gives of the strength Christians can be in the body of Christ. Each one of us is different, just as each part of the body is different. So, each of us has a different function to perform. We should never be too proud of our abilities nor should we ever think we have nothing to contribute. The Christian community is composed of a diverse group of people, from various backgrounds, with different talents and abilities. It could be easy for our differences to divide us, but we have one thing in common - faith in Christ. Each person is important. In the analogy of Paul, if a seemingly insignificant part of the body is removed, the whole body will be weakened and less effective. Therefore, we should not look down on those we think are not important, nor should we be envious of those who seem to have more impressive abilities. We are part of the body, and as such it is important that we fulfill our role to enable the Christian community to function at full strength.

Teamwork is a necessity in the Christian life. All of us have different abilities and interests, but each function that is performed is important. Some may think that the person who gets up in front of the group and speaks each week counts for the most. But who is to say that speaking is more important than a person who quietly takes soup to an ill person or shares a cake with a shut-in? In fact, Christ emphasized the importance of sharing a glass of cold water, visiting in prison, clothing the naked and feeding the hungry.[33] This is what Martin Luther called "the priesthood of all believers." He was saying that everyone is important in the team of the Christian community and each can play the role of a priest by ministering to others in his own unique way.

God relates to us as members of a team. The scriptures say "We are workers together with God."[34] God works, we work, and we work together with God.

God puts into our hands what we could never create and says to us, "Here, do something with this." For example, I love to raise tomatoes. So I take a tomato seed, which I cannot make, and I plant it. I can plant, tend and fertilize. And in three or four months, we have a harvest of nice, tasty, red tomatoes. We? Yes, God and I. I do what I can - plant, tend, and fertilize. God does what I can't - provides seed, rain and sunshine. And working as a team we get the job done.

We are blessed that God allows us to be on His team. What we are able to do may not seem significant, such as giving encouragement, sharing a glass of cold water, or tending to a tomato plant. Perhaps God could have organized the world in such a way that we humans weren't needed at all, but He didn't. He invites us to be workers together with Him. What a privilege to be on His team, and to experience His presence in the struggles of the game, as we share in His eternal victories.

In basketball and the Christian life, there can be little success unless each person believes in and works together to accomplish the same goals, while genuinely appreciating the success of others. That's the awesome privilege of sharing in the community of a team.

STYLE

Finding your personal style is a rich journey of discovery, wonder, adventure and excitement.

Alexandra Stoddard

In matters of grave importance, style, not sincerity, is the vital thing.

Oscar Wilde

Cultivate your own capabilities, your own style. Appreciate the members of your family for who they are, even though their outlook or style may be miles different from yours. Rabbits don't fly. Eagles don't swim. Ducks look funny trying to climb.

Chuck Swindoll

To paraphrase Oscar Wilde: In basketball and the Christian life, style is the vital thing.

One of the most interesting ways to watch a basketball game is to observe the various styles of play. Some teams attempt to run the fast break every time they have the ball. Other teams want to "slow the game down," passing the ball six or seven times before a shot is taken. Many teams run set plays, while others primarily let their offense develop, based on the defense the opponent has in place.

There are several defensive styles, including the man-to-man and the zone, with variations of each. Some teams press all over the court, while others may press at the half-court line, setting traps when the ball goes to a corner. A zone defense makes it difficult to defend the three-point shot, but keeps the big men from scoring "inside the paint." Most teams will change their style of defense several times during a game, depending on the circumstances and the players on the floor.

Generally, when fans talk about players on a basketball team, they mention their style of play. Are they exciting? Do they hustle? Can they hit the jump shot or the outside shot? Do they play good defense? Do they block out for rebounds? In fact, style is the most significant component of a basketball team, as well as the Christian life.

What do you consider to be the most important and revealing aspect of your life? Is it your heritage, your possessions, your reputation, or your potential? It is none of those. The most decisive aspect of your life is your style.

Often, people who seek to know about Jesus ask about His looks, His physical size, His weight, or the color of His eyes and hair. That kind of information is not helpful in understanding Jesus. The only way to really know Him is to understand His style.

For example, there was the occasion when Jesus met a woman of Samaria at a well. His disciples were surprised that He would even speak to her. You see, Jews never associated with or even spoke to Samaritans, based on some old prejudices that dated back many years. In addition, this woman had been married several times and was currently living with a man who was not her husband. Naturally the disciples thought it unusual that Jesus would talk to such a woman. But He spent time with her, listening, talking, showing concern, and even asking for a drink of water.[35] What else could He do? That was His style.

Then, there was the time when Jesus had been teaching and preaching all day, healing the sick and giving sight to the blind. He was very tired. Children were brought to Him that He might touch them. The disciples tried to make the parents take the children away, but Jesus said, "Let the little children come to me, and do not forbid them, for of such is the Kingdom of Heaven."[36] Jesus loved children. It was His style.

Look at Golgotha, where Jesus was hanging on the cross suffering pain of mind and body. On the ground below the soldiers were gambling for His clothing. Jeers and taunts were being shouted at Him by the crowd. In the midst of this Jesus prayed, "Father, forgive them, for they do not know what they are doing."[37] What manner of man is this who forgives the people who are killing Him? But God's Spirit was in Jesus' heart. What else could He have done? It was His style.

It is interesting to observe that Jesus often sought to authenticate who He was by directing attention to His style. John the Baptist had announced Jesus' coming. But when John was thrown into prison, he began to doubt that Jesus was the long awaited Messiah. John told some of his followers to go to Jesus and ask Him directly, "Are you the One who was to come or should we expect someone else?" The answer Jesus gave directly pointed to His style. He told John's disciples to go back and report what they had seen and heard. Namely, that the blind receive their sight, the lame walk, the lepers are made clean, the deaf hear, the dead are raised, and the good news is preached to the poor.[38] That was Jesus' style.

Jesus was not only mindful of His own style, He was also concerned about the style of His followers. He told them to let their light shine before others who would see their good works and give glory to their Father who is heaven.[39] He even expected the style of His followers to be that of loving their enemies.[40] He said that His followers should bless those who curse them, do good to those who hate them, and pray for those who persecute them.[41] He told them to pray in secret to God, and not to pray elaborate prayers in order to impress other people.[42]

The style of the Christian life was established and

demonstrated by Jesus. The style of a basketball team is determined by the coach. If the players refuse to mold to his style, they will not get in the game. Likewise, we must realize the only valid way to determine if we are true disciples of Jesus Christ is whether we are living by His style. Church membership and conventional morality are not enough. We must have His style. This is the only portrait many individuals will see of the Christian life. People aren't concerned about seeing more buildings, or parades, or displays of institutional power. Neither do they care about dogmas, rituals, ecclesiastical statements, or ceremonies. People who seek to be part of the Christian life, more than anything else, want to know, "Do Christians live by the style of Jesus? Do they serve other people, forgive their enemies, and live in the spirit of love?" That is the ultimate test.

Can we say with the Apostle John, "We know that we live in Christ and He in us, because He has given us of His Spirit"?[43] The Spirit of Christ living in us is what enables us to live the Christian style.

What is the most vital factor of a basketball team and of a follower of Christ? It is style!

HOME COURT ADVANTAGE

Teams win more games on their home floor. Some advantage comes from familiarity with physical characteristics—-the floor, the lighting, the air conditioning—-but much of it comes from the fans.

Ricky Byrdsong

It is an advantage for a team to play basketball on their home court. Many years ago one of the main reasons for this advantage was the lack of official dimensions for the floor and each place to play was unique. The writer, James Michener, described the gymnasium where he played in his youth. "The baskets were hung flat against the end wall, and a player could get hurt if he drove hard for a lay-up. The ceiling was low, making it difficult to put an arc on a shot. The court was so unusual that it took opponents more than half of the game to familiarize themselves with the peculiar floor."[44] Michener and his teammates had a real home court advantage in those days.

In the 1950s and 1960s high school and college gyms were greatly improved, but no official dimensions had been adopted yet. In addition, the floors had their own peculiarities, such as dead spots. This, of course, gave the home team a real advantage. They knew where the dead spots were and stayed away from them when they were on offense. On defense, however, they would closely guard a player who was unfamiliar with the floor. When he dribbled the ball on the dead spots, it was easier to steal the ball.

Berea College is a small liberal arts school in Kentucky. A book, using the oral statements of various players, tells the history of Berea basketball. One of the players describes the home court advantage the Berea College team had in the 1950s:

"To win at home, it's not the basket or the familiarity with the floor, not that sort of thing at all. It's about ninety percent the support of the crowd. It's a psychological thing. You're loose, you feel good, and you feel like when you shoot, it's going in. And more of them do when you feel that way. Our gym, (Seabury) was a good gym. However, you had to be very careful on a corner shot. There was an overhead running track, an oval. Anywhere out on the floor you were okay; it didn't really cause a problem. But that overhanging oval cut off the corners of the rectangular basketball floor and you had to know where to shoot and where not to shoot. If you got back in the corner, you could easily catch the edge of that overhang." [45]

Today, even though all basketball courts have official dimensions, playing on the home court is still an advantage. Statistics of college basketball games show that teams have a higher winning percentage on their home court than on the opponent's court. Professional teams play an eighty-two game schedule. The teams are highly motivated to achieve a good record in the regular season so they will enjoy a home court advantage in the playoffs. The teams that have the best regular season records will play four playoff games on their home court and three games on the opponent's court. Statistics are overwhelming that teams win more games playing at home. Why is this so?

Ricky Byrdsong, head basketball coach at Northwestern University, asked his players why they thought they won a higher percentage of their games at home. They gave him three reasons.

First, they were familiar with the surroundings at home. They knew the arena, the people who cooked their food and the people who cleaned the locker room. In addition, they were able to sleep in their own beds the night before the game. When a team is on the road, a great deal of energy and thought goes into coping with an unfamiliar environment.

Second, a team has a great feeling of confidence when they play at home because they believe they will be treated fairly. When playing on the road, players feel the officials tend to favor the other team. Good referees do not go into games intending to favor one team over the other. When a team is playing at home, the officials know there is pressure to be extremely fair because the people in the stands have a vested interest in the game. Fans know the game today, and they will loudly disapprove of sloppy calls by officials.

Third is fan support. Most players would rather be cheered than booed. The home fans support the players when they make a good play and even when they make a mistake. On the road, however, the opposite is true. If a visiting player shoots a ball that misses everything, the chant begins: "Air Ball! Air Ball!" Every time that player touches the ball the "Air Ball" chant is raised. Fans at home will also support their players when they are down. It is easy to cheer for a team that is playing well: scoring baskets, blocking shots, pulling down rebounds and winning games. But encouraging fan support is needed most when the team is down.

Ricky Byrdsong makes the insightful statement that the locker room can be a home court advantage when the team is on the road. In the locker room players can be themselves, enjoy team banter, tell jokes, and get their bearings. Before the game, the locker room is where the coach helps the team to focus on the game. At half-time, the locker room is the place where the team can regroup.

After the game, the locker room is the location where the team celebrates victory or deals with the disappointment of defeat.[46]

Being at home is important in basketball, but it is even more vital in daily life. In 1999 the San Antonio Spurs won the National Basketball Association World Championship. For ten years, their 7'-2" center, David Robinson, had anticipated this day. When the final seconds ticked off the clock at the Alamo Dome and the Spurs had finally won the championship, the fans rushed onto the court. Amid all the excitement, a photographer took a picture of David Robinson hugging his young son. Later, when Robinson was on the "Tonight Show with Jay Leno," he spoke of what a special moment that was. The Spurs had spent a lot of time on the road during the season, and this particular game would be the final one of a seven-game series against the New York Knicks, providing they won. If they lost, however, they would have to travel to New York and play one more game. David Robinson had told his son that if the Spurs won, he would be home and the two of them could spend time together. The crowd rushed onto the court to celebrate the world championship. But when David Robinson's son ran on the court to hug his dad, he was celebrating that his dad was coming home, and they could be together.

There is a "home court advantage" in life because at home everything around you is familiar. The routines are familiar: milk and cookies after school, a kiss and a hug after getting a scraped knee, and the smell of supper cooking on the stove. The places are familiar: the kitchen where everyone gathers, the back yard where the children play, and the table where the family gathers for meals and conversation. The people are familiar: parents, siblings, grandparents, relatives, and neighbors who drop by to visit.

Another "home court advantage" is that people are treated fairly and respected for who they are. Charlie

Shedd told of Dennis, who was a mechanical whiz and almost a genius at repairing bicycles. In elementary school, when all of his friends were working for good grades, Dennis was taking his scooter apart. By junior high, he was working on bicycles with gears and handbrakes. His mother and father were educators, but that was not for Dennis. So when Dennis was in high school, his parents told him, "Son, we would really like to see you graduate. We're not going to be on your back about grades. We are proud of the way you can do things we can't do. We think you're great. We just want you to be you." Now he owns a big bicycle repair shop, and his parents look at education in a different way. They believe that each child should be treated fairly by being educated according to their ability to succeed, rather than fitting into a standard mold set for everyone.[47]

Another "home court advantage" involves the support that is received. John McMaster was a superstar basketball player in high school, making All-Conference and All-State. In his senior year he was named the Most Valuable Player in the league. Every year he played, his mother never missed a game, at home or away, regardless of the weather or travel distance. She was always in the bleachers, cheering for her son even though she was totally blind. Although the mother could not see her son, he could see her, and that support made all the difference.[48] Support requires love, time, and giving of self. The Apostle John wrote: "Our love should not be just words and talk; it must be true love, which shows itself in action."[49]

There are also techniques to creating a "home court advantage" away from home. When our children were small, I was the pastor of a busy, fast-growing church. Most of the responsibilities for parenting were carried by my wife. From the time our children were three and six, until they were teenagers, however, I took each of them, individually, on a monthly outing. We would go to their favorite place to eat, we would do what they wanted to do, and we would talk about their interests or concerns. It was an amazing and fulfilling experience. When it was time for their monthly outing, no matter what they were doing, they were excited about going out and being alone with their Dad. A bonding took place that is strong to this day. Growing up is tough, but when a child can share the joys and disappointments of life with a parent, and there is no one around to interfere, that is the true gift of a "home court advantage."

One summer my wife and I traveled out west. On Sunday we found ourselves in the mountains of Arizona, worshipping in a beautiful little church. That day the pastor concluded her morning prayer by saying, "We pray all of this in the name of Jesus Christ, who came and lived among us, and who died on the cross for us, and who rose from the dead, so He might take us to our eternal home." I thought, "Wow! God really does want His people to have a "home court advantage." Then I remembered how this idea is expressed in Scripture and in Christian music.

When David wrote the 23rd Psalm, he concluded by saying, "Your beauty and love chase after me every day of my life. I'm back home in the house of God for the rest of my life (forever.)"[50]

On the night before Jesus was crucified, he said to his disciples: "Don't let this throw you. You trust God, don't you? Trust me. There is plenty of room for you in my Father's home. If it weren't so, would I have told you that I'm on my way to get a room ready for you? And if I'm on my way to get your room ready, I'll come back and get you so that you can live where I live."[51]

Then I remembered some of the old Gospel and spiritual songs.

Softly and Tenderly
Softly and tenderly Jesus is calling,
calling for you and for me;
See, on the portals He's waiting and watching,

watching for you and for me.
Come home, come home, ye who are weary, come home.
Earnestly, tenderly, Jesus is calling, calling, O sinner,
come home!

Amazing Grace
Through many dangers,
toils and snares I have already come.
'Tis grace hath brought me safe thus far,
and grace will lead me home.

Swing Down Sweet Chariot
Swing down sweet chariot and let me ride,
Rock me Lord, rock me Lord, calm and easy.
I've got a home on the other side.

This "home court advantage" gives us confidence and support in our earthly home as well as our heavenly home. In our family, every night before we go to sleep, we say to each other, "Good night. I love you. And I'll see you in the morning." One evening Betty Jane and I returned home from a meeting, to find a note on the kitchen table from our daughter, who was then eight years old. The note said, "Dear Mom and/or Dad, I want to take my lunch to school tomorrow, but I can't find the peanut butter and we don't have no jelly. Good night, I love you and I'll see you in the morning." When my wife saw that note, she immediately went to work to make a sandwich for our daughter's lunch. But she didn't make a peanut butter and jelly sandwich. She made the best submarine sandwich imaginable, filled with meat, tomatoes, sauce, lettuce, onions - all kinds of good stuff. Our daughter, who had gone to sleep in the confidence that her situation would be handled by her mother better than she could handle it herself, awakened to find that wonderful sandwich. It was something she could never have imagined or have made by herself.

When it comes time for our bodies to die, we will know that we did all we could, and we will say to our loved ones, "Good night. I love you. And I'll see you in the morning." When we awaken in heaven, we will find that the scriptures and the songs of the faith are right. Christ really did prepare a place for us in God's home. And it won't be anything we could have made for ourselves, like a peanut butter and jelly sandwich. As with the submarine sandwich for our daughter, the place prepared for us will be far more wonderful than we could ever imagine.

That's why the Scripture says, "No eye has seen, no ear has heard, no mind has conceived what God has prepared for those who love Him."[52] The Scripture further promises, "When this tent we live in - our body here on earth - is torn down, God will have a house in heaven for us to live in, a home He Himself has made, which will last forever."[53]

A "home court advantage" is tremendous. And just think. We can enjoy it in basketball and we can enjoy it in life. And God promises that we will enjoy it forever.

JUST PLAIN THIRSTY

Fluid, salt loss, and body heating retard physical performance. Even a slight amount of dehydration causes physiological consequences. For example, every liter of water lost will cause the heart rate to be elevated by about eight beats per minute.

Matt Hermes

It was a hot June day in Florida, the kind of day a person can get thirsty simply walking around. Our daughter had just graduated from college, and she had a job, so we were out looking for a car she liked and could afford. After a couple of hours of going from dealer to dealer she said, "Let's stop and get something to drink." I replied, "No, we have to keep going until the job is done." She said, "Dad, I'm really thirsty." I replied, with a great aura of "mature" knowledge, "Well, I'm from the old school. When I used to play basketball, we never drank water until practice was over." She responded, "We know a lot more now, Dad. It's not a good thing (interpretation: it's not smart, or a better interpretation: it's dumb) to exercise or make decisions when you are just plain thirsty." She bought something to drink, but I was too hard headed to follow suit. Of course, it has become one of those family jokes now, about Dad being of the old school. I decided that I should get on the internet to do some research and much to my amazement she was right. They have learned a great deal since my days of playing basketball.

One person wrote that it is just pure stupidity not to keep players hydrated. The easiest way to prevent heat injuries is to drink water or sports drinks. Both are helpful, but in different ways. Water is more easily absorbed by the body, and facilitates getting oxygen into a person's system, while getting carbon dioxide out, thus preventing dehydration which causes muscle cramps. Sports drinks, however, replenish cells with carbohydrates, electrolytes and other minerals lost due to dehydration.

If your body is inadequately hydrated, it can also affect your cognitive ability. Basketball is not only a game of high-intensity running, but of skill, concentration and decision making. Those last factors are impaired both by dehydration and lowering of blood-glucose levels, both of which are helped by sports drinks. The good news is that basketball offers many opportunities to hydrate during the game including time-outs, quarter or half-time breaks, and time spent on the bench. Practices should also be organized to allow for drink breaks. Each player should have his own drink bottle courtside, so he can keep track of how much fluid he is receiving. Players should constantly take sips of water throughout practice, just enough so they are not thirsty. Then, immediately after practice, it is important to replace carbohydrates in a liquid form.[54]

Keeping hydrated with the proper liquid is a necessity in high intensity basketball. The University of South Carolina performed a study involving two groups of basketball players who were put through a strenuous workout that included shuttle runs, a twenty meter sprint, and a whole-body motor skills test. One group of players was given a carbohydrate-electrolyte sports drink during rest periods throughout the test, while the other group was given flavored water that looked and tasted the same. The members of the sports drink group were able to run 37 percent longer on average, ran faster in the twenty meter sprint, and performed better on the motor skills test.[55]

Jesus was often "just plain thirsty." His life, teaching, and ministry were carried out in Galilee, Samaria, and Judea, all of which were hot and arid. He often spoke about the blessing of receiving a drink of cold water,[56] and he did not hesitate to ask for some water when he was thirsty.[57] He even described His teachings as being water that He gives to people so they will never be thirsty again.[58] He understood what people felt when there was a severe shortage of water in the body, causing muscles to tighten up, short-circuit and eventually cramp.

Because we have had similar experiences, we find ourselves strongly drawn to a statement Jesus made when He was hanging on the cross. That statement is "I thirst."[59] According to Scripture, Jesus made seven statements while He was hanging on the cross: three that focus on His relationship to God and three that center on His relationship to people. This statement, however, which is the fifth statement, stands out. It seems odd, almost vulgar, even selfish. His concern is for Himself, for His own body. If ever there was a time when He seemed to utter purely self-absorbed words, there they are: "I thirst."

There are those who do not interpret these words by their direct, simple meaning. They believe that Jesus was speaking symbolically, saying, "I thirst, I yearn for the living God." What an abstract, unrealistic understanding of these words! Jesus had not slept all night, a crown of thorns had been placed on His head, He had been beaten with a leather whip that had metal tips, He had been forced to carry a heavy cross through the streets of Jerusalem, nails had been driven into His hands and feet, and He had been hanging on the cross in the hot sun for three hours. He was just plain thirsty, as any of us would be. If an athlete's body can become dehydrated just from playing basketball, imagine how dehydrated Jesus' body was. I believe people are too quick to give "spiritual" meaning to Jesus' words, "I thirst," and in doing so fail to comprehend their significance.

Let me explain. Many people prefer to think of Jesus as being God at a masquerade ball, going through the motions of being a man, but free of the common trials and torments of humanity. They do not want to believe that He was completely a human being, but this is not the Christian belief. The Christian belief is that Christ, the second person of the Trinity, became a human being. He was born as a little baby, nursed at His mother's breast, and saliva ran out of his mouth like other babies who are cutting teeth. He was weaned and learned to walk, talk, read and write. He had a nervous system, just as we have. When He walked a long way, He became tired; when He had nothing to eat, He became hungry; when He was hot, He became thirsty; when He was sad, He cried; and when nails were driven into His hands and feet, they hurt, and He bled. In other words, He was completely a man.

Jesus was not God in a human mask. He was as fully man as He was fully God. He came to reveal to us what God is like and He did this very clearly. But He also revealed to us what we are meant to be as human beings, showing us the type of life God wants us to live.

Why do some people hesitate to take the words, "I thirst," at their face value? Is it for the same reason that so much religious art shows Jesus as a pale, effeminate young man whose physical existence is almost make believe? We just don't want to believe that Christ was completely a man who dared to live on earth under the same circumstances as we live. We would rather think of Him with our own preconceived notions, not in the way He is portrayed in Scripture. Read Matthew 23 and you may be surprised to learn that Jesus called the Pharisees a brood of vipers and white-washed tombs, full of putrid and decaying flesh.[60] The idea that Jesus had endless patience is not supported in the Scripture. He said to Peter, who did not seem to understand what He was doing, "Out of my sight, Satan! You are a stumbling block to me; you do not have in mind the things of God, but the things of men."[61] He had no patience with the money changers in the temple, who were taking advantage of the people. He started a one man riot, driving the money changers out of the temple, and shouting at them, "Get out of here! You have made my Father's house a den of thieves. It is to be a house of prayer!"[62]

Jesus was not thinking about spiritual matters when He said, "I thirst." He was just plain thirsty. So what's the difference and what does that statement from the cross mean to us? I suggest three things.

First, God is very serious about us and our eternal salvation. The reason we have not allowed ourselves to believe that Christ was completely human is because it is so much easier for us to think that He just appeared to go through the motions of being a man, but He really did not suffer. It is a very sobering thing to understand that Christ loved us so much that He was willing to be whipped, spit upon, nailed to a cross, and left to die. These words, "I thirst," are the simple assurance that God was not playing a game when Christ came. He was not like some wealthy visitor from the "right" side of the tracks who schedules a brief tour through the slums to distribute Christmas baskets. He made His homes in the slums, so to speak, enduring everything - the poor food, the dirt, the bugs, the daily trials of life. This is part of what is implied when Christ says, "I thirst." This is how far God will go to forgive us and grant us eternal life. When we understand that we know we need to take Him very seriously.

Second, the statement "I thirst" means that Christ knows and understands what we go through in our daily lives. The One to whom we pray knows what we experience, because He has been there. He understands our temptations. He has felt our discouragement. He is touched when we tell Him there is more to do than can ever be done. He smiles when we confess our weariness. He understands long, tiring days, and what it means to be "just plain thirsty."

Third, do you wonder what happened when Jesus said, "I thirst?" He was asking for help from the men who were torturing Him, intending to kill Him. Why should they bother to do anything? Perhaps a few were sympathetic, but they did nothing. There was one man, however, who was moved to action. He seemed to say to himself, "This man, Jesus, has had nothing to drink for over a day, and He is suffering a great deal. If I do not help Him now, I will never be able to do so because the end is very near." So the Scripture says that he ran to help.[63] We don't know this soldier's name. He was so busy doing his act of kindness that he failed to leave his autograph. We may envy him because he had the opportunity to serve Christ in His final moments.

But you and I have the same opportunity every day to serve Christ because, figuratively speaking, He is still on the cross. His suffering on the cross represents the heartache that He has for people who are suffering today. He is still being crucified through the agony and poverty of those about us. Christ once said, "I was thirsty and you gave me a drink. Because you have done this to one of the least, you have done it to me."[64] So we have the privilege today of serving Christ by reaching out in love to those who are hurting, hungry and thirsty.

"Just plain thirsty." Three words which are so basic, so common, so daily. But they remind us of the importance of a drink of cold water in a basketball game and in our Christian lives. For those who thirst for the love expressed in the receiving of Christ, there is good news. He will give you living water and you will never be thirsty again.

Second Best

It is 1979, a basketball game in the Brandeis gym. The team is doing well, and the student section begins a chant, "We're number one! We're number one!" Morrie, (a professor at Brandeis,) is sitting nearby. He is puzzled by the cheer. At one point, in the midst of "We're number one!" he rises and yells, "What's wrong with being number two?" The students look at him. They stop chanting. He sits down, smiling and triumphant.

Mitch Albom, Tuesdays With Morrie

Everyone wants to be the best, to be on the first team. But what about the players who are sitting on the bench? Can they benefit from the experience of being second best?

Some players are on the second team because they matured later than others. While they are sitting on the bench they have an opportunity to learn more about the game and its values. Basketball teaches many things including competitiveness, the significance of fundamentals, how to deal with stress, the importance of teamwork, respect for authority, and the fun of the game. These are values that will be beneficial in life, and can be learned well, even while playing on the second team.

Non-starting players are very important to a team. Some of them relish their role of working hard in practice, particularly in scrimmages, because they know they are making the whole team better on game night. Some "second best" players have earned the very important role of playing 10 to 12 minutes a game, giving the starters an opportunity to rest.

Coaches have found a variety of ways to show appreciation to non-starting players. For example, when Dean Smith was the coach at the University of North Carolina, he formed the Blue Team, which was composed entirely of substitutes. The men on the Blue Team knew they were going to play for two minutes in the first half of very game. When their time came, they always hustled, played hard-nosed defense and unselfish, team-oriented offense. This was a tremendous boost for team morale and had a positive effect on practices.[65]

Because no competitive player is content with being second best, he is constantly working to improve his game and self-image. College Coach Harry Sheehy believes that the best method for improvement is by the setting of appropriate goals. He does not feel it is appropriate for a player to set a goal to work hard so he can become a star or be on the starting five. A player may never achieve the goal of being a starter, causing him to become frustrated and quit. It is better to set a goal of working hard in order to improve his game and benefit the team. A work ethic that improves the team also helps the individual with the later challenges of life.[66]

Individuals who do not play a great deal help to develop the star players and should be appreciated. Everyone on the team has a valuable role to play. When John Wooden coached at UCLA, there was a press conference after every game. He could almost predict what questions the media would ask and what players they wanted to interview. He always tried to use this opportunity to praise the individuals whom the media would overlook. He would say, "When I put so-and-so in just before the half and he made that steal, it quite possibly could have been the turning point in the game." He wanted every player to know they were important, and that players on the second team should never feel their efforts were wasted in the star's shadow.[67]

Our society needs to realize that an individual or

a team can be successful without being number one. In 1967 the University of North Carolina was playing in a consolation game in the NCAA basketball tournament. Disappointed that they had lost the semi-final game, the consolation game was a real let-down. They were losing by over 20 points. Suddenly, with five minutes left to play, the North Carolina fans began to chant, "We're Number Four! We're Number Four!" The chanting revived the spirit of the team, and they realized that a number four finish in the national tournament was quite an accomplishment and something to celebrate.[68]

Wanting to be number one seems to be everyone's desire, whether in basketball or the Christian life. In the Gospel of Matthew, there is the story of Salome, the mother of James and John, who goes to Jesus, and kneeling before him, says, "All I want is that you allow my sons to be number one in your kingdom. I want one to sit on your right hand and the other to sit on your left." She wanted what she thought was best for her sons, but her ambition showed that she did not understand what Jesus and His kingdom were all about. Jesus told her that there are going to be great people in His kingdom, but they won't be determined by the standards of the world. He suggested it would be better for her boys if they played second fiddle. Then Jesus said, "Whoever wants to become great among you must be your servant, and whoever wants to be first must be your slave—-just as the Son of Man did not come to be served, but to serve."[69] Servants do everything for the good of others, not to make themselves first.

George Bernard Shaw said that the most difficult instrument in the world to master is second fiddle. The world does not understand it, or appreciate it, or reward it, but the second fiddle is a beautiful instrument when played with the right attitude. Not everyone in an orchestra can play first fiddle. In fact, the contribution of the person who plays first fiddle is small compared to the proportion of those that make their contributions on other instruments to the total effect of the orchestra. The caliber of a performer is indicated not by the place he occupies or the instrument he plays, but by how well he performs in the niche that is his. A second fiddle can spoil the entire performance if played poorly, or can add beauty and quality if played properly.

I suppose it is our society's emphasis on number one that makes us focus in on the apex when we look at a pyramid. But the apex is not the entire pyramid. Ninety-nine percent is the sustaining base beneath the highest point. There would be no apex were it not for the dependable foundation that holds it up. The ultimate strength of any institution or team lies in the humble, out-of-sight people who are committed to do their part the best they can because they are committed to the good of all.

It should also be said that very few of us have the opportunity to live our lives on the basis of our first choice, but on what we consider at the time to be second best. Whistler, the great artist, started out to be a soldier, but failed miserably at West Point because he could not pass chemistry. Phillips Brooks, the great Boston minister, who wrote "O Little Town of Bethlehem," studied to be a teacher, but he was a complete failure. Sir Walter Scott, the great novelist, planned to be a poet.

In the book of Acts, there is the story of Paul and his determination to go to Bithynia and preach the Gospel. Bithynia was one of the richest provinces of Asia Minor and to carry Christianity there would have been very significant, but Paul was not allowed to go. Instead his plan was broken and he went to Troas.

The book of Acts describes it this way: "When they came to the border of Mysia, they
tried to enter Bithynia, but the Spirit of Jesus would not allow them to. So they passed by Mysia and went down to Troas."[70]

Going to Troas was second best to Paul. He was

not a half-way person. He wanted very much to go to Bithynia, but the Spirit wouldn't let him go. That is a way of saying that circumstances changed his plans. So Paul went to Troas, the second best, and it became one of the greatest opportunities of his life. Why?

First, Paul believed that God had a purpose for his life, and if God had led him to Troas there must be something there worth discovering. Likewise, God has a purpose for your life. When you find yourself in what you consider to be second best, even this can work for good. Paul found that to be true, and he would later write, "And we know that in all things God works for the good of those who love him, who have been called according to his purpose."[71]

Second, Paul's concern for people enabled him to make a difference in Troas. Too often when we find ourselves in a "second best" situation, we pity ourselves. Whoever we are and in whatever situation, if we care about people and apply the values of teamwork, including humility, sharing, responsibility, and joy, we can turn that "second best" situation into victory.

God had something wonderful in store for Paul at Troas. There he had a vision of a man from Macedonia in Greece, who was calling for help. If Paul had gone to Bithynia he may never have had that vision and the Gospel might never have spread to Europe. God's "No" to Bithynia became an open door to Europe.

Has God ever said "No" to you? By the shattering of Paul's dream, and putting him in a "second best" situation, a new door opened, a new day dawned and a new vision emerged. And God can do the same for you.

The Bible tells the story of Joseph who was sold into slavery by his brothers and was later untruthfully accused of rape by his master's wife. What a "Troas," what a "second best" that was. Yet God brought him out of prison to be reunited with his brothers to whom he declared the remarkable words: "You meant evil against me, but God meant it for good."[72] That was his Troas. That was his "second best." But God meant it for good.

It is hard for us not to want to be number one, whether in basketball or in life. But if we're willing to serve the human team of which we are a part, and to trust that God is working something out for our good, then we will not only be following in the footsteps of Jesus, but we will be considered great in His kingdom.

WHAT IS BETTER - PAST OR PRESENT?

No one cares what happened in last year's Finals. Fans just want something they can get excited about, have fun and make their own holiday.

Mark Cuban

This is the worst basketball being played since I can remember, and it's not because I'm an old guy. Is it because it's a generation gap, or is it because they aren't doing it right?

Charles Barkley

A favorite topic of conversation in every generation is, "Was life better in the past than it is today? Were athletes better in the old days than they are now?

Of course, today's athletes believe they are the best, and they document the reasons why: they are bigger, they can jump higher, they have been taught better shooting techniques, and they compete in a game of basketball that is more advanced than the game of the past. People who played in "the good old days" have a different opinion. They say that athletes in their era were tougher, more disciplined, never questioned the authority or directions of the coach and had a stronger loyalty to their team. In fact, they say that sports in general were better back then. Maybe so. Maybe not.

Sure, twenty-five or so years ago it cost less than a month's rent to buy a ticket for a college or professional basketball game. Players weren't trying to make statements by putting tattoos on their bodies. Ball players would sign an autograph without expecting to be paid. All of that is good.

But was it really better twenty-five years ago? There was no all-sports radio, fantasy basketball had not been invented, the National Basketball Association draft was not televised, and ESPN did not exist. Most of the sports news was about local teams, and if you ever moved away, it was a struggle to follow your favorite team.

Tickets were cheap, but sometimes the seats were behind a huge pillar and often there were no backs on the seats. There was seldom any halftime entertainment, nor was there a mascot jumping around, adding fun for the spectators. Occasionally the games were televised, but seldom in color. There was no instant replay, the score was not on the screen and statistics were not given. Basketball was not as exciting in those days, before dunking became cool and the three point shot made it possible for a team to come back from certain defeat.

Worst of all, basketball players wore those tight little shorts that looked like underwear. That alone should convince us that basketball really was not better twenty-five years ago.

I played on the basketball team and ran track at a small liberal-arts college more than twenty-five years ago. During that time I remember talking with an alumnus of the college, who described in great detail how much better the teams were in his day than in mine. I resented that. I notice, however, that as I grow older and remember my playing days, I seem to be so much better in my mind now than I was in actuality. And I know that the teams on which I played were better than teams are today.

What is it about us, whether we are talking about basketball, business, or life, that makes us want to glorify the past and the successes we had - or think we had?

The Apostle Paul, writing to the people at Philippi said, "I concentrate on this: I leave the past behind and with hands outstretched to whatever lies ahead I go straight for the goal."[73]

Paul is making two points. First, we should not dwell on the things that are behind. They are over. Paul had every reason to brag on his past victories and accomplishments. He was highly educated and was a member of the elite in society. Other than Christ, no one in the Christian movement has ever come up to his achievements. But Paul is saying that the Christian cannot rest on his or her laurels and constantly dwell on past achievements.

The best selling book *Tuesdays With Morrie* tells of the relationship of Morrie Schwartz, a retired college professor, and Mitch Albom, one of his students from nearly twenty years earlier. Morris is dying with amyotrophic lateral sclerosis (ALS,) often called Lou Gehrig's Disease. Mitch visited Morrie in his home every Tuesday, and they turned their rekindled relationship into what they called "one final class about lessons in how to live." Each Tuesday there would be a different subject. One week they discussed why people, as they age, always look to the past and want to be young again.

"Morrie smiles and says, 'You know what that reflects? Unsatisfied lives. Unfulfilled lives. Lives that haven't found meaning. Because if you've found meaning in your life, you don't want to go back. You want to go forward. You want to see more, do more.'

'Listen. You should know something. All younger people should know something. If you're always battling against getting old, you're always going to be unhappy, because it will happen anyhow.'

'Mitch, it is impossible for the old not to envy the young. But the issue is to accept who you are and revel in that. This is your time to be in your thirties. I had my time to be in my thirties, and now is my time to be seventy-eight.'

'You have to find what's good and true and beautiful in your life as it is now. Looking back makes you competitive. And age is not a competitive issue.'"[74]

What a liberating idea! Whether in life or in basketball, we're all going to get older, and we don't have to compete with those who are prominent in the arena today. Our past is gone, and the opportunities that were ours in those years are now alive in someone else. We have the opportunity, in basketball and in life, to "leave the past behind." Our task is to stop trying to be competitive in our own minds about how successful we were and to follow Morrie's advice to "find what is good and true and beautiful in life as it is now."

Second, Paul is saying that we should "go straight for the goal." He seems to be describing a distance runner straining to reach the finish line. Past laps do not matter. The goal ahead is all important. We are to concentrate on the challenges and opportunities of today.

Berea College is a liberal arts school that offers no athletic scholarships, but competes successfully against colleges that do give scholarships. In the early 1960s, however, they experienced several losing seasons. Many people longed for the glory days of earlier years. Some wondered if Berea should begin to give athletic scholarships and change their unique program. Jerry Trammell, a student who wrote an article in the *Berea Alumnus* entitled, "Whatever Happened to the Old Ball Team?" ended his comments with these words:

"Athletics, properly directed, strengthen character and establish necessary traits of leadership and self-confidence that help enable the participant to later assume the role of a useful and productive citizen. Certainly this is the primary aim of the Berea College Athletic Department. Any person knows that if an athletic program can fulfill these goals and aspirations, then that program is worth the effort and time and money that are put into it. We will continue to put out teams as long as there are Berea men with the determination to play and win."[75]

To strengthen character, establish traits of leadership, develop self-confidence, and be a useful, productive citizen is the goal of athletics and the way to a meaningful life. In order for this to happen, it is important that "with hands outstretched to whatever lies ahead, we go straight for the goal." We must understand that today belongs to God, just as tomorrow belongs to Him. Often we are so concerned about future possible events that we miss the opportunities for the present. God has promised to give us strength and loving support for the present moment.[76] We will never know that we have this strength and loving support until we actually begin to go straight for the goal. We will put more value on living fully in the present moment if we realize the value God puts on it. He has such a high regard for time that He gives only one moment at a time, and does not give us the second moment until He has withdrawn the first.

We have been given a fabulous gift. We are able to leave the past behind, with all of its competitiveness and "with hands outstretched to whatever lies ahead," live each day to the fullest, assisted by God's strength and loving support. Just think! We are invited to participate fully in life, whatever our age may be. We don't have to embellish stories of how good we were in the past. Who we are today is what matters.

And best of all, we don't have to wear those tight shorts.

Unknown but Important

*All the gold in the world couldn't buy the prize
given the 1936 Olympic edition, the very first US basketball
team. That group of unknowns earned more than gold;
they each earned a handshake and a laurel of wreath from
the inventor of basketball, James Naismith himself.*

Brad Herzog

Most of the individuals who have made
contributions to the game of basketball are relatively
unknown, whether they are coaches, players, referees
or administrators. Likewise, most people who have
been involved in the Christian life are unknown, even
though they serve faithfully on the mission field, in small
churches, in hospital emergency rooms or provide shelter
for homeless people. Even though none are well-known,
all have made an important difference.

Luther Gulick is one such person. Most people
know that it was James Naismith who invented the game
of basketball, but it was Gulick who prompted him to
do so. Naismith had just received a degree in theology
from Presbyterian College in Montreal. He had always
been interested in sports, however, so he decided to go to
Springfield, Massachusetts, and study physical education
as a graduate student. He was thirty-one years old at the
time. Part of his graduate program involved instructing
other students in various physical fitness activities. In
the summer there was baseball and in the fall there was
football, but it was very boring in the winter. Gullick, who
was superintendent of physical education at the school,

challenged Naismith to create "an indoor game that would be interesting, easy to learn and easy to play in the winter by artificial light." So Naismith, after trying several other games, finally drew up 13 rules, put a basket on each end of the gymnasium, and the game of basketball was invented.[77] Everyone knows the name of James Naismith, but few know about Luther Gulick. Yet, without Gulick, the game of basketball would not have been invented.

Danny Biasone is another relatively unknown person who made an important contribution to the game. In the 1940s and early 1950s, basketball was marked by stalling tactics. For example, on November 22, 1950, the Fort Wayne Pistons beat the Minneapolis Lakers 19 to 18. The two teams combined to score only eight baskets in what is the lowest scoring game in NBA history. In games like that, players would stand around, holding the ball, and not even try to score. They would wait until they were fouled and then take their free throws. Games became free throw contests, and were very boring to spectators. Danny Biasone, owner of the NBA's Syracuse Nationals, developed the 24 second shot clock to speed up play. The simple idea was that the offense would have to attempt a shot and hit the rim within 24 seconds or lose possession of the ball. Biasone's clock was tested in the summer of 1954 and adopted for use in the 1954–55 season. As a result, scoring and excitement were brought back into the game. Danny Biasone had this to say about his idea: "Basketball needed a time limit. In baseball you get three outs. In football you have to gain 10 yards in four plays or you give up the ball. But in basketball, if you had the lead and a good ballhandler, you could play around all night. The number of seconds really wasn't that important. No matter what, the game needed a time element."[78]

Trainers, physical therapists and equipment managers are generally unknown to the public, but are of great value to the team. Trainers and physical therapists help the players stay healthy and deal with injuries. Many of them have some medical training that is put to good use in keeping their players in top playing condition. A person even less known is the equipment manager. His job is to make sure that everything the team needs, such as uniforms, towels, socks and shoes, is available at home or when the team is traveling.

In Christianity, as in basketball, there are many people who are not well known who have made a significant contribution to the faith. One such Biblical person was Onesiphorus. Evidently he had no special qualities that enabled him to do anything outstanding, but he was extremely grateful to have become a Christian under the influence of Paul. Later, when Paul was in prison, wearing chains, some of his friends deserted him, but not Onesiphorus. He visited Paul and performed common deeds of friendship. He could not have known how he was needed by Paul, nor could he ever have guessed how much his influence would affect the future. In Paul's second letter to Timothy he wrote:

"May the Lord show mercy to the family of Onesiphorus, because he cheered me up many times. He was not ashamed that I am in prison, but as soon as he arrived in Rome, he started looking for me until he found me. May the Lord grant him his mercy on that Day. And you know very well how much he did for me in Ephesus."[79]

Onesiphorus probably never knew what his life meant to Paul and thus to Christianity.

Then there was the boy, who was listening to Jesus teach, standing on the edge of a crowd, feeling so very small among so many. He had his lunch with him - five small barley loaves and two small fish. The crowd was hungry and the boy was willing to give his lunch to Jesus. The Master took the loaves and fish, gave thanks, and multiplied them so that everyone had plenty to eat. There were even twelve baskets of food left over by those who had eaten.[80] Think of what this boy, through Christ, was able to do for all of those people. His name was never recorded. But even though he is nameless, he has such a significant place in Jesus' ministry that his story continues to be told today.

A theme runs through these stories of little known people who have made significant contributions to basketball and to Christianity. It reminds us that there are unexpected ways in which ordinary folks like us are needed. We may never know the person who is helped. We may never guess the consequence of our words or deeds today. Remember Onesiphorus. He simply went to see a friend who was in chains. God has promised to bless us when we do such small things as give a drink of cold water to a stranger, visit the sick, clothe the naked and feed the hungry, even if no one knows about it but the one who receives.

> This crowd on earth
> They soon forget
> The heroes of the past.
> They cheer like mad
> Until you fall
> And that's how long you last.
>> But God does not forget
>> And in His Hall of Fame
>> By just believing in His Son
>> Inscribed you'll find your name.
> I tell you, friends,
> I would not trade
> My name however small
> Inscribed up there
> Beyond the stars
> In that celestial hall.
>> For any famous name on earth
>> Or glory that they share.
>> I'd rather be an unknown here
>> And have my name up there.[81]

We may not be well known here on earth, and few may know our name, but God knows who we are and the contributions we have made. That's all that's important. In fact, the only thing that matters is to one day hear our Savior say, "Well done, good and faithful servant. You have been faithful with small things. Enter into the joy of the Lord."[82]

Same Concepts and Terms

Naismith's focus was the total man, though basketball was obviously the most-recognized part. But he was also a chaplain, a man with a religious degree and Christian background, and a man with a medical degree.

John Gosset

James Naismith, the inventor of basketball, had degrees in theology and physical education. It is no accident, therefore, that basketball and the Christian life use many of the same terms and maintain similar concepts.

Time-Out

Most basketball players are tall, muscular people, who run the floor with smooth, fluid motion. Many of their plays are based on timing, but sometimes they "get out of sync" and nothing is accomplished. When that happens, the coach will call a time-out. Often the coach will allow the players to be still for a moment. Then he talks to them, sometimes quietly, sometimes passionately. The players relax, take a deep breath, and join hands in a huddle. They have had a moment to reflect, to be reminded of what they are supposed to do, and they go back into the game with a new sense of determined purpose.

Jesus often took time-outs, going off by Himself to pray.[83] He encouraged His followers to do the same thing, telling them to go into a closet, close the door and pray in silence.[84] In the hectic pace of life, we need to take more time-outs to be still, allowing the Lord, our Coach, to speak to us, reminding us of who we are, what we are about and where we are going. Then we can re-enter the game of life with a new sense of determined purpose.

Get the Right Equipment

The properly equipped basketball player uses a mouth guard, wears compression shorts and has ankle support, such as tape. The mouth guard helps to shield the teeth, but its primary purpose is to keep the mouth closed to protect the tongue. Compression shorts provide protection against muscle strains during activity while keeping thigh muscles warm during rest periods. Ankles should be taped for each practice or game, keeping them from turning and lessening the risk for a sprain or break. If shoes are properly fit, blisters on the feet can be prevented. Braces are supportive for players with chronic knee problems. Wearing the proper equipment is necessary to play the game well and to reduce the occurrences of injury.

People of the Christian way must also have the right equipment to confront life's challenges. A good study Bible, with commentary, life applications, background information, book introductions and cross references is a requirement. Hymnals, with a variety of music including classic, Gospel, contemporary and praise songs, provide for an understanding and strengthening of the faith. Growth and inspiration are supplied through devotional materials on the subject of Christian living. It is impossible to escape the difficulties and hurts of life, but having the proper equipment that enables faith to grow deeper will provide the strength to overcome challenges and heartaches.

Helping a Person Up

When Dean Smith was coaching at the University

of North Carolina, if one of his players fell to the floor drawing a charge, or went flying across the court going after a loose ball, his teammates were expected to rush over and help him up. They did this because they understood the player was sacrificing his body for the rest of the team. Even in practice, the coaches would run to help a player up who was on the floor after drawing a charge.[85]

Infants are content to roll across the floor and crawl to reach something they want, but that doesn't last very long. They are driven to be upright, to reach higher, and to find their way in the world. No matter how many times they fall, they continue to get up. They do not want to see the world from their knees. Human beings have been created to risk and try again. Even though most of us can pick ourselves up after a fall, nothing helps the healing process or makes the next step easier than a steady, strong hand reaching out to assist. In the Christian life we offer our hands to those who have fallen, to help remind them they will stand again. The hymnist Fanny Crosby wrote, "Weep o'er the erring one, lift up the fallen. Tell them of Jesus, the mighty to save."[86] God is in the business of helping us up when we're down. The Psalmist wrote, "God lifted me out of the slimy pit, out of the mud and mire; He set my feet on a rock and gave me a firm place to stand."[87]

Assist

In basketball, an assist is a pass to a teammate which leads directly to a basket. Players who average seven to ten assists per game generally do not make a lot of baskets, but their unselfish play enables their team to score points and be successful.

People who give assists are equally important in the Christian life. Jesus told a story about a man who was beaten up, robbed, and left lying beside the road. A priest and Levite passed by but they did nothing for the injured man. A Samaritan, however, saw him laying there and assisted him by giving him first aid, bandaging his wounds and taking him to an inn for the night. Jesus said this man was the real neighbor because he gave the assist.[88] Nobody got his name. He wasn't a big scorer, but his assist changed everything for the injured man.

One-on-One

In basketball, when an individual offensive player maneuvers against a defender, he is said to be going "one-on-one."

Jesus did some of His best teaching in one-on-one situations. For example, Nicodemus came to Him by night, and Jesus shared with him, one-on-one, the opportunity for new birth through the moving of the Holy Spirit.[89] Jesus went one-on-one with Zacchaeus, a hated tax collector, whom he saw up in a tree, when He invited Himself to his home for supper.[90] The Christian faith is shared most effectively when it is communicated one-on-one.

Self Confidence

Ricky Byrdsong, who was head basketball coach at Northwestern University, says that at the start of every season and before every game is played, a coach gathers his players to give them encouragement and help them to believe in themselves. He tells them that each player is valued as an individual and that they are capable of accomplishing the goals of the team. One player may be a tremendous scorer, another a great rebounder, a third an excellent passer, and another a strong defender, but each one is important. The team will be successful when each player has self-confidence, knowing his importance to the team and the coaches.[91] Before every University of Kentucky basketball game, Coach Tubby Smith shakes the hand of each player, an act which says, "You are important, I believe in you, and we are unified as a team."

For nearly twelve years I was the Chief Executive Officer of Penney Retirement Community, a facility established by J. C. Penney in 1926. I learned a great deal about this famous merchant and the many problems he faced. He went broke during the Depression, which forced him to live in only one room of his house and to can his own food. He also experienced physical and emotional illnesses for which he had to be hospitalized. When asked about the struggles of his long life he replied, "I am grateful for all my problems. As each one was overcome, I became stronger and more able to meet those yet to come." Mr. Penney was a man of faith and he found that the Bible is filled with practical ideas that give us self-confidence. "If you can believe, all things are possible to him that believes."[92] "Ask and it will be given to you; seek and you will find; knock and the door will be opened to you."[93] "For God did not give us a spirit of timidity, but a spirit of power, of love and of self-discipline."[94] With self-confidence and God's help, we can be victorious.

The Concept of Threes

Coach John Wooden looked at basketball as a game of threes. Forward, guard, center: the three basic positions in the game. Shoot, drive, pass: the three fundamental skills needed on offense. Ball, you, man: when playing defense a player (you) must be aware of his man and the ball. Conditioning, skill, teamwork: the three foundations of playing successful basketball.[95] There are other ways the number three is significant in basketball including the three-point basket, (a shot from behind an arc that extends around the basket,) and the three-second violation, (a rule that forbids an offensive player from standing longer than three seconds inside the painted lane closest to the basket.) In recent years, Phil Jackson, the successful professional coach, has installed an offense called "The Triangle," which seeks to create undefended spaces on the court. The system gets its name from one of its most common patterns of movement, the sideline triangle.[96]

The Christian life is filled with the concept of threes. The prophet Micah said that God has three requirements: "What does the Lord require of you? To act justly and to love mercy and to walk humbly with your God."[97] In his famous chapter on love, the Apostle Paul gives a list of three things that will always remain: "And now these three remain: faith, hope, and love. But the greatest of these is love."[98] Christian theology teaches that God has revealed Himself in three ways known as the Trinity: Father, Son, and Holy Spirit. William Barclay, famous Biblical scholar, states that there are three rules for life. First, we must never be self-centered in our happiness because there are others who are in pain. Second, we must never be selfish in our prosperity. Third, we must never be self-righteous in goodness, because the self-righteous person is furthest from God.[99] Some of the most importance concepts for living can be found in threes.

Keep Your Head Up

It is imperative for a basketball player to keep his head up as he runs the floor, dribbles the ball and looks to pass the ball to an open teammate. Keeping his head up is also crucial in grabbing rebounds of missed shots. Coaches will often tell a player who has made a mistake to keep his head up, not to get discouraged because the team needs him to have a positive attitude.

Keeping your head up is important in the Christian life. Norman Rockwell has a famous painting depicting a beautiful church building. People are walking past with their heads down, oblivious to the uplifting worship taking place inside. A well-known speaker who saw the painting wrote a speech entitled, "Lift Up Your Eyes." The Christian faith causes us to lift up our eyes, to see that there is more to life than walking around with our heads down, as if we are looking for a coin or counting the cracks in the sidewalk. A minister went to Europe and was so entranced with all of the castles that he wrote a sermon about them. As he started to deliver his sermon, he looked out in the congregation and saw a woman who made her living washing floors and washing clothes for people. He felt badly about what he was saying. How could this woman relate to castles? After the service was over, as the people were leaving the church, this woman came to the minister and said, "I really appreciate what you said today, because it made me forget those terrible dirty floors and wash tubs I work with every day." One purpose of the Christian faith is to remind us to keep our head up, even through the trials of daily life.

Helpful terms and strengthening concepts for basketball teams and the Christian community include: take timeouts; get the right equipment; help a person up; assist others; be involved one-on-one; have self confidence; look at life in threes; and keep your head up.

Trash-Talking

Perhaps more than ever before, athletes and coaches are divided on what constitutes acceptable behavior on the court. I am not alone in my opinion that trends such as excessive celebration, taunting and trash-talking are detrimental to sports on all levels.

Tom Fakehany

Trash-talking - a term that includes boasts, insults, put-downs, taunts, and threats - has become a big part of basketball and the Christian life. Athletes participate in sports to demonstrate skills, to execute what has been learned, and to share in the accomplishments of teamwork. Talking trash contributes to none of that. People participate in the Christian life to share in community, find purpose in life, worship God and experience forgiveness for their sins. Talking trash and gossip contributes to none of that.

Some think that trash-talking in basketball is a way to get an advantage over an opponent, because it makes him feel badly about himself, question his ability and lose his temper. A few coaches even encourage trash-talking, thinking it makes the opposing player lose concentration. What it often does, however, is prevent the player who is talking the trash from being able to concentrate on his own game.

Many see trash-talking as a decline in sportsmanship and as another sign of society's general loss of civility. When a player resorts to trash-talking in an effort to defeat an opponent, he is admitting he can't win using his own physical and mental abilities. It is totally inappropriate to curse an opponent or make negative comments about his skin color or ethnic origin. In addition, trash-talking takes away from the team because it focuses on the individual. It is an illustration of our modern society in which the emphasis is upon "me" rather than "we."

Taunting and in-your-face trash-talking causes fights and slowly deteriorates the ideas of sportsmanship and fair play.

To be fair, it should be said that some trash-talking is done in fun, to get into a player's psyche. In game one of the 1997 NBA Finals, the Utah Jazz and the Chicago Bulls were tied at 82. Utah's Karl Malone (known as "The Mailman," because it was said he always delivered), was fouled with nine seconds left to play. If he made one of the two free throws, the Jazz would be in a good position to pull off a first game upset. Malone missed the first shot. Before the ball was returned to him for his second shot, Scottie Pippen, who played for the Bulls, went over to Malone and whispered, "The Mailman doesn't deliver on Sundays." Malone missed again and the Bulls won the game.[100]

Trash-talking is becoming an integral part of most sports talk shows. While much of it is out of control, some of it is humorous. When Charles Barkley was an active player, he was always outspoken, but as a television analyst of the National Basketball Association game, he is even more colorful. In the 2004 playoffs, the Los Angeles Lakers had a team of stars, two of whom were Karl Malone and Gary Payton. Barkley said of them, "Karl Malone and Gary Payton were great in their day, but they're not in their day."[101]

Teams are often surprised when trash-talking turns out to be detrimental to them. Trashing-talking to the media about an opposing player or team often stimulates the opposition to play harder. Statements appear in the paper and the coach hangs the article on the locker room wall for all to see. Trash talking through the media does little more than anger and motivate the opposing team.

Basketball teams need charismatic players, but that charisma should be shown in athletic ability, team play, hustle, and the joy of the game, not in trash-talking.

Too much talking often leads to surprising results, as seen in the story of John and Agnes. They had been courting each other for eighteen years. John could never find the courage to ask Agnes to marry him. One day they were taking a ride in the car when John decided to pop the question. Agnes modestly accepted his proposal of marriage. They drove for several miles, without another word being spoken. Finally Agnes said, "John, don't you have anything sweet to say to me?" John replied, "No Agnes, I have said too much already."

Whether in basketball or in the Christian life, one of our biggest problems is saying too much. The Bible speaks often of the harmful effects of talking trash.

"Keep your tongue from evil, and your lips from speaking lies."[102]

"Be careful what you say and protect your life. A careless talker destroys himself."[103]

"A fool's mouth is his undoing, and his lips are a snare to his soul."[104]

"If anyone considers himself religious and yet does not keep a tight rein on his tongue, he deceives himself and his religion is worthless."[105]

"No one has ever been able to tame the tongue. It is evil and uncontrollable, full of deadly poison. We use it to give thanks to our Lord and Father and also to curse our fellow-man, who is created in the likeness of God. Words of thanksgiving and cursing pour out from the same mouth. My brothers, this should not happen!"[106]

"Whoever would love life and see good days must keep his tongue from evil and his lips from deceitful speech."[107]

Trash-talking is effortless and seems to be harmless, but nothing has more critical consequences than words that are said. Jesus made that clear when He stated, "I tell you that men will have to give an account on the day of judgment for every careless word they have spoken. For by your words you will be acquitted, and by your words you will be condemned."[108]

As children we learned the saying, "Sticks and stones can break my bones, but words will never hurt me." Is that saying really true? A little boy was being harassed by a bigger kid, who called him names, insulted him, and made fun of his family. The little boy went home, crying to his mother. She told him, "Those names and insults can't hurt you. You go back and tell that bully, that bigger kid, that 'sticks and stones can break my bones, but words will never hurt me.'" So the little boy went back and said, with all the conviction he could muster, "Sticks and stones can break my bones, but words will never hurt me." Then he thought for a moment and said, "And that's a big lie." If you get hit with a stick, it hurts and puts a lump on your head for three or four days, but the lump will go away. A big rock may break an arm, causing excruciating pain, but that arm will get set and in six weeks can be used again. But when someone says, "You're stupid, you cannot do anything right, you're ugly," those wounds may fester for years. Negative criticism and insensitive comments can do harm for a lifetime.

An older man saw an advertisement about hearing aids that could not be seen when they were worn. He decided he would try one. The arrangement was that he could wear it for two weeks, and if it didn't drastically improve his hearing, he could return it. After two weeks he returned to the store and said, "This thing is wonderful." The person behind the counter replied, "I'm sure your family enjoys you having that hearing aid, don't they?" "Oh no!" he exclaimed. They don't even know I have it. I've really had a ball. They don't know I can hear what they say. In the last two days alone, I have changed my will twice." Many things we say will echo back to harm us.

It is important to encourage, congratulate and support those individuals who conduct themselves in the proper manner. In order for this to happen, people must change from within. The root problem is not in the mouth, but in the heart. Jesus said, "The good man brings good things out of the good stored up in his heart, and the evil man brings evil things out of the evil stored up in his heart. For out of the overflow of his heart his mouth speaks."[109]

All of us should ask God each day to change our hearts and help us to live by these words: "I will not let any unwholesome talk come out of my mouth, but only what is helpful for building others up according to their needs, that it may benefit those who listen."[110]

Trash-talking belongs in the trash, not in the game of basketball or in the Christian life.

Let Go of the Missed Shot

The only important shot you take is the next one. Because no matter ho hard you try, that is the only one you can still have an effect on!

Jason Bumblis

What to do with a mistake—-recognize it, admit it, learn from it, forget it.

Dean Smith

Letting go of a missed shot is a major challenge in basketball and in life. To do so, however, contributes to success in the present and in the future.

What type of player would you want to take the last shot of a game, when the championship is on the line and there are a few seconds to play? Would you prefer the player with the best statistics and the highest scoring average? The television commentators seem to think so. When the game is on the line, they give the statistics of the best free throw shooter and the leading scorer. Then they say that one of those two probably will take the final shot. Another factor that needs to be considered, however, is how well a player reacts to pressure. Pressure motivates some players to perform above their abilities, but causes others to tighten up or choke. So what type of player is best suited to take the final shot when the championship is on the line?

Jonathan Niednagel, who in the sporting world is known as the "Brain Doctor," claims to know the answer. Niednagel has spent thirty years researching genetics, neuroscience, and personality profiling, as well as observing athletes. In this process he has identified sixteen brain types, each of which he has labeled with a four letter acronym borrowed from the psychiatrist, Carl Jung. Each type represents a different combination of physical and mental strengths and weaknesses. Niednagel insists that there is a connection between brain types and physical performances.

For example, Niednagel says that the player with the brain type "ISTP," which stands for Introversion, Sensing, Thinking, Perceiving, is the type of player who is more likely to be successful when the game is on the line. This player sees only the task at hand and attacks it with fearless precision. Feelings, such as the thought of an earlier missed shot, the elation of winning, or the painful disappointment of losing, seldom get in the way.

According to Niednagel's research, in the National Basketball Association there are five other brain types that are most prevalent. One of the most common is the "ISFP," an acronym for Introversion, Sensing, Feeling, and Perceiving. This player is wired very much like the ISTP with one big difference. He is subject to the emotion of the moment. He tightens up when the pressure is on because he remembers an earlier missed shot. He cannot let go of the negative thoughts, making him a poorer risk to take the last shot.

At first thought it may seem ridiculous to classify athletes into brain types. Yet more than twenty professional teams from various sports contract the services of Niednagel, paying him many thousands of dollars to seek his insights that will help them determine which athletes have the brain chemistry to handle pressure and be winners.[111]

In basketball conferences where the athletic ability is strong and evenly matched, it is important for a team to have as many players as possible with the ISTP brain type. Why is an ISTP brain type preferred over an ISFP? An ISFP brain type may be the leading scorer on the team, but he is a *feeling* person, who pounds the ball in frustration when he makes a mistake and is surely aware of how many shots he has missed when he takes the one that decides the game. On the other hand, the ISTP is the type of player who does not dwell on his mistakes, and even though he may have missed twenty shots during the game, his mind is clear as he concentrates on making the game winner. He has let go of the negatives that have been part of his game, and he is clearly focused on the task at hand.

One of the reasons Michael Jordan was such a successful basketball player was that he clearly focused on the task at hand. He said,

"I never looked at the consequences of missing a big shot. Why? Because when you think about the consequences, you always think of a negative result. I can see how people get frozen by the fear of failure. They get it from peers or from just thinking about the possibility of a negative result. They might be afraid of looking bad or being embarrassed. That's not good enough for me. I realized that if I was going to achieve anything in life, I had to be aggressive. I had to get out there and go for it. I don't believe you can achieve anything by being passive. I know fear is an obstacle for some people, but it's an illusion for me."[112]

So, if you want to be successful, who would you choose to take the final shot? It surely must be the player who is not afraid, who lets go of past mistakes and who concentrates on making the final shot that will win the game. Letting go of blunders and mistakes is necessary in order to be successful in basketball and in life.

Letting go of missed shots (sin and wrongdoing,) is crucial in the Christian life. The Apostle Paul is an example. Early in his life his entire focus was on destroying the Christian movement, stalking Christians in order to put them to death. However, as he was walking along the Damascus Road one day, he had a dramatic experience with the risen Lord and his life was changed completely. Not only did he become a believer, but he became a leader in the church, traveling from place to place, telling of God's gift of forgiveness and eternal life in Christ Jesus. Because of the wrongdoing of his past, he easily could have been too overcome with guilt to function. But he became a type of pioneer missionary and was the most prolific writer in the New Testament. Writing a letter to the Christians at Philippi, he said, "I am still not all I should be, but I am bringing all my energies to bear on this one thing: forgetting the past and looking forward to what lies ahead, I strain to reach the end of the race and receive the prize for which God is calling us up to heaven because of what Christ Jesus did for us."[113] Paul is saying that even though he "missed the shot" in the past by doing harm to the Christian community, he is letting go of that and using all of his energy to tell of God's love, forgiveness, and eternal life in Christ Jesus.

Peter was one of Jesus' disciples who often missed important shots. On one occasion he bragged that he would never deny Jesus, even if everybody else did.[114] Yet, when Jesus was on trial, Peter did deny him three times, until he finally said to a little servant girl as they were standing around a campfire, "I don't know who this man is."[115] After Jesus was crucified and had risen from the dead, He met Peter beside the Sea of Galilee. He forgave Peter for his denials, and then Jesus gave him the responsibility of caring for His followers.[116] Seven weeks later, on the Day of Pentecost, Peter stood before a crowd at Jerusalem and preached such a powerful sermon that three thousand people became believers and were baptized.[117] Peter could have become so overcome with despair at denying his Lord that he would never again try to speak on behalf of Jesus. He let that go, however, and preached a sermon so powerful that the Christian movement was impelled on its way.

Throughout my life I have enjoyed the game of basketball more than any other sport. In high school, however, I felt my coach was unfair to me and to others. After graduation my contempt toward him festered and grew. I thought I had a right to my feelings because I had been mistreated. About ten years after graduation, I went back to my high school to watch a basketball game. I saw my coach on the other side of the gym, but I did not want to speak to him. He, however, walked across the floor to greet me and to ask about my life and family. I realized that he was unaware of my feelings toward him, and they weren't hurting him at all, but were like venom in me, causing painful damage. I saw the necessity to let go of my hostility. I went home and wrote him a letter, asking forgiveness for my attitude toward him. By return mail, I received a handwritten response, in which he said he was shocked at the feelings I had described, and that all was forgiven. It was a tremendously joyful relief to let go of the missed shot of a broken relationship.

Learning to let go and forget is very important in our every day relationships.

"If you see a tall fellow ahead of the crowd,
A leader of music, marching fearless and proud,
And you know of a tale whose mere telling aloud
Would cause his proud head to in anguish be bowed,
It's a pretty good plan to forget it.

If you know of a skeleton hidden away
In a closet, and guarded and kept from the day
In the dark; whose showing, whose sudden display
Would cause grief and sorrow and lifelong dismay,
It's a pretty good plan to forget it.

If you know of a spot in the life of a friend (We all have
spots concealed, world without end)

Whose touching his heartstrings would sadden or rend,
Till the shame of its showing no grieving could mend,
It's a pretty good plan to forget it.

If you know of a thing that will darken the joy
Of a man or a woman, a girl or a boy,
That will wipe out a smile or the least way annoy
A fellow, or cause any gladness to cloy,
It's a pretty good plan to forget it.[118]

God has made us in such a way that when we miss a shot, in whatever area of life it may be, we have within us the ability to let that go and move on. In Maxwell Maltz's book *Psycho-Cybernetics,* he states that we can form the habit of remembering past successes and forgetting past failures. This is the way the human brain is supposed to work. It would seem that people who are learning to shoot a basketball would never be able to hit the target, because as they learn they repeatedly miss the goal. If repetition was the answer to improving skill, practice would make us experts at missing, since that is what we have practiced the most. But that is not how God made us. The computer in our brain remembers and reinforces the successful attempts, while forgetting or letting go of the misses. The reason many of us do not succeed is that emotionally we impress on our minds our failures and forget about our past successes. Maltz states, "It doesn't matter how many times you have failed in the past. What matters is the successful attempt, which should be remembered, reinforced and dwelt upon."[119] God has made us in such a way that we can let go of the missed shots of our failures, and in our minds, discern that we can be more than we are.

Letting go of a close, loving relationship, when it is necessary, is extremely difficult. It may be a teenage romance or a relationship later in life. The one who has been in our thoughts constantly, who has brought much joy and excitement, is no longer going to be there. At first we may deny the need to let go. We desperately try to hang on and to keep love alive. When that doesn't work, we finally understand that we need to find a way to let go. Only then can we begin to move forward to the next stage of life. Letting go of close relationships takes courage, but when that is necessary it is essential to place our trust in God, whose love will never let us go.

George Matheson was engaged to be married when he discovered that he was slowly but surely going blind. When his fiancée learned of his condition she came to the painful decision that she could not face life married to a blind man. Out of his suffering, in having to let go of the girl he loved so deeply, he came to understand more clearly the love of God. George Matheson wrote:

"O Love that wilt not let me go
I rest my weary soul in Thee;
I give Thee back the life I owe,
That in Thine ocean depths its flow
May richer, fuller be."

Letting go of missed shots is crucial to the basketball player and to the Christian. In the challenge of letting go, we have the assurance that there is One - even God Himself - who will never let us go.

Be There for the Team

Eighty percent of success is showing up.
Woody Allen

All he did was show up, but his presence was the difference between victory and defeat. Willis Reed, center for the New York Knicks, limped onto the floor two minutes before game seven of the National Basketball Association Finals on May 8, 1970, in what has become one of the classic games of basketball.

In the first four games of the finals against the Los Angeles Lakers, Reed had averaged 32 points and 15 rebounds per game. In the fourth quarter of game 5, however, his right leg sustained a serious injury in the form of a torn abductor muscle. The Knicks managed to hold on and win that game, by the score of 107 to 100. In game 6, however, playing without their injured center, the Lakers overpowered them, 135 to 113. The Lakers' seven-foot-two Wilt Chamberlain, who many think was the most dominating center to ever play the game, scored 45 points and grabbed 27 rebounds. Now the series was tied at three games each, and the final game would be played at Madison Square Garden. Even though it would be a home game for the Knicks, they seemed to be doomed to failure because of the injury of their leader and center.

During the warm-ups in the Garden, star Laker players Elgin Baylor, Jerry West, and Wilt Chamberlain, limbered up for what they surely must have thought would be their first championship together, because Willis Reed could not play. The Knicks fans at the Garden were hopeful, but almost resigned to defeat as their team, without their star center, took the floor for their pre-game practice. Before the game, however, Reed had been given shots of carbocaine and cortisone. Two minutes before tip-off, he made his way out of the tunnel into the arena, dragging his right leg behind him. The crowd went wild and the confidence of his teammates seemed to return. Bill Bradley, starting forward for the Knicks, wrote that when Willis appeared from underneath the stands, the audience erupted in a roar as loud as Niagara Falls. The advantage shifted and each Knick felt uplifted. Dave DeBusschere, the other starting forward, recalled that the opposing team stood at the other end of the court, their warm-up stopped, just watching Willis, his lips pursed in determination, taking his shots before the game's opening buzzer.[120]

When the game started, Reed somehow managed to get the opening tip over Chamberlain. Reed then scored the first basket of the game on a shot from the top of the key. A minute later, he made a second shot from the same spot, putting the Knicks permanently into the lead. Those were his only shots of the game. As the game wore on, the pain in Reed's leg increased. Because he had made those two early shots from outside, Chamberlain was forced to come to the top of the key and guard him. This left the low post open, allowing the Knicks to work their plays. The Knicks were ahead 29 points before halftime, and won the game by the final score of 113 to 99.

It was such a dramatic moment that Murray Janoff of The Sporting News wrote: "Willis Reed may be the first guy to ever win a game by merely showing up. Statistically, only four points in fifteen minutes. But . . ."

Reed's own teammates and coach had the same conviction. "Just Willis' presence was a psychological lift for us," exclaimed Walt Frazier. Red Holzman, head coach of the Knicks, said that Reed's presence made a difference. "He gave us a tremendous lift just going out there. He couldn't play his normal game, but he meant a lot to the spirit of the other players."

Willis Reed, however, did not think that highly of himself. He said, "That's something a lot of people put a lot into to achieve. It wasn't something just for Willis Reed, it meant something to the team, the fans, the coaching staff."

Willis Reed's words and actions reflected the spirit of the Scripture:

"Therefore, I urge you, brothers, in view of God's mercy, to offer your bodies as living sacrifices, holy and pleasing to God - which is your spiritual worship. By the grace given to you I say to every one of you: Do not think of yourself more highly than you ought, but rather think of yourself with sober judgment, in accordance with the measure of faith God has given you."[121]

If Willis Reed had decided to sit out the final game, it would have been understandable. He knew he was putting himself into a situation where there would be pain, struggle and difficulty, but he wanted to be there for his team. He could have basked in the glory of the first five games, with his exceptional scoring and rebounding statistics. But he gave up all of that and lessened his averages to be present for the team.

This is exactly the spirit and motivation Jesus Christ had when he came into the world to be present with us. The Bible says:

"In your lives you must think and act like Christ Jesus. Christ Himself was like God in everything. But He did not think that being equal with God was something to be used for His own benefit. But He gave up His place with God and made Himself nothing. He was born to be a man and became like a servant. And when He was living as a man, He humbled Himself and was fully obedient to God even when that caused His death - death on a cross."[122]

The good news of the Scripture is that Jesus Christ

cared enough about us to be there for us - to be present for us. Helmut Thielicke expressed it this way:

> "Jesus Christ did not remain at base headquarters in heaven, receiving reports of the world's suffering from below and shouting a few encouraging words to us from a safe distance. No, He left the headquarters and came down to us in the front-line trenches, right down to where we live and worry about what our enemies might do, where we contend with our anxieties and the feeling of emptiness and futility, where we sin and suffer guilt, and where we must finally die. There is nothing He did not endure with us. He understands everything."[123]

Today, the resurrected Christ continues to be with us where we live, as we struggle with emptiness, anxiety, guilt, and uncertainty. A young man, whose father had suddenly died, was thrust into being the president of his father's company. He was not prepared for it and he did not understand what he was supposed to do. He began to pray that some peace might come to him and some guidance might come that would help him be more effective in running the company. He said that one day it happened. He received the peace and guidance for which he had been praying. His first thought was that his father was trying to relate to him, but he quickly realized that he was experiencing the presence of the resurrected Christ.

That story would not have made sense to me if it had not been for a similar experience of my own mother. She was going through the most difficult time of her life, causing her to contemplate suicide. She said that one night, when she was in the depth of despair, she felt the presence of the resurrected Christ at the foot of her bed. Suddenly, she was at peace and the turmoil left her. The presence of the resurrected Lord brings peace and understanding in the midst of anguish.

One of the greatest opportunities of the Christian

life is to "be present" where we are, and to share the presence of the resurrected Christ where there is pain, loneliness, hunger and need. But what does "being present" really mean?

When we were in elementary school and the teacher called the roll, we would either say "here" or "present." But were we always really "present?" Maybe we were only physically present, because mentally we were thinking about a ball game that afternoon. Or maybe we were half-asleep because we stayed up too late the night before watching television. We hoped the teacher wouldn't call on us because we were not prepared. The teacher, however, hoped we were really present so we could learn the day's lesson. Then, later when we were thirteen or fourteen, a person of the opposite sex suddenly became very present to us. That person had always been there, we saw them, but never before had that person been present in such a vivid way.

Being present where we are means not being preoccupied. In fact, one of the ways mental illness is described is by saying, "they're not all there." When Jesus was facing death on the cross, he asked three of his disciples to go and be with Him as he prayed at the Garden of Gethsemane. They went with him and they were physically present, but they went to sleep. Three times Jesus came back and said, "Can't you stay awake for me for just a little while?"[124] He was asking, "Can't you be present with me?"

Life has many situations in which it is important for us to be present. When our children come to us with problems we need to be present and listen attentively to them, rather than escaping into ourselves saying, "I sure will be glad when they get bigger so I won't have to deal with all of this." When we are at work it is important for us to really be present rather than thinking, "I can't wait until I can retire." People often need someone to be present with them as a supportive friend. Alcoholics Anonymous is an example. Every member of that organization has a sponsor or friend who promises, "Whenever you need me, wherever you need me, I'll be there." Being a friend means being present when you are needed.

Prayer is another area of life where presence is critical. We know that God is always present with us, but sometimes we are so busy or loud that we cannot feel Him. When we follow His instructions to "Be still and know that I am God,"[125] His presence comes flooding into our lives. The amazing thing is that through the gift of intercessory prayer, when we pray for others, we can sometimes feel their presence more vividly than if they were physically in the room. Many times when we are in their physical presence, we talk about trivial things and avoid getting below the surface. But if there is a friend we know is going through real difficulties, when we pray for them, their presence is more intense than if we were actually sitting across the table.

Ray Smalley, a retired agricultural missionary, and Willis Reed, an injured basketball player, had the same commitment - to be present, to be there for the team. You know Willis Reed's story. Here is Ray Smalley's story.

Ray Smalley lived in a Florida retirement community where I served as the chief executive officer. This facility had its own on-campus church, at which the residents were responsible for worship and all activities.

Ray was a resident in assisted living. Even though he was in declining health, he felt it was important to be physically present in church every Sunday for worship. He could have watched the services via closed circuit television in the activity room of the building where he lived, but that would have meant just sitting and observing and he wanted to be really present. It was not a simple matter of Ray getting up, shaving, taking a bath, walking to church and returning to his room after worship. It was a long process. Someone had to shave, bathe and dress him. Then an independent living resident would bring him to church, support him as he walked down the aisle to his seat and sit with him during worship.

Ray Smalley never wanted attention for himself. He just wanted to be there for the team. He could not hear or understand everything that took place. But when he was present, the most meaningful part of the worship service occurred as the first stanza of the closing hymn was sung. Ray Smalley, with great difficulty, began walking slowly down the center aisle, holding the arm of the person who brought him, making his way out of the church.

As this feeble, elderly man shuffled along, tears would swell up in people's eyes. Here was a man who had served his Lord and made his contribution to God's kingdom. It would have been easier for him to stay in his room, but he wanted to be there for his Lord and His team. He never said a word and he was unable to participate fully, but his presence was an inspiring, strengthening influence.

The importance of presence - of being there for the team. Willis Reed, who in the midst of struggle and pain was there for his team, is the example in basketball. Jesus Christ, who left the glories of heaven to be present for us, and struggled in pain on the cross, is the example in life. It is our privilege to be present where we are, to be there for others, and to share the presence of the resurrected Lord.

(Footnotes)

[1] John 15:16 Ph

[2] John 15:11 Ph

[3] John 15:12–13 Ph

[4] John 15:16 Ph

[5] Luke 15:11–20 Msg

[6] Luke 23:42–43 (My paraphrase of the story.)

[7] I Peter 2:9–10 Msg

[8] Pat Conroy *My Losing Season,* Nan A. Talese, an imprint of Doubleday, New York, New York, 2002, Page 40

[9] Ibid., Page 41

[10] Found this quotation without a footnote or end note in the following booklet: John C. Maxwell, *Teamwork Makes The Dream Work,* J. Countryman, a division of Thomas Nelson, Inc., Nashville, Tennessee 2002, Page 97.

[11] Pat Conroy, Ibid., Page 398

[12] John C. Maxwell, Ibid., Page 23

[13] Internet, Ai3Net.com, "Lifestory."

[14] Time Magazine, January 31, 2005, pages 58–59, Article by Sean Gregory

[15] Internet, Resources on Hope, Message by Tony Campolo, "Trusting in God in the Days that Lie Ahead."

[16] Psalm 61:2 NIV

[17] Hymn, Higher Ground, Tune by Johnson Oatman, Jr.; text by Charles H. Gabriel, found in many hymnals , including *Hymns For The Family of God.*

[18] Jeremiah 18:1–7 NCV

[19] "Have Thine Own Way, Lord" by Adelaide A. Pollard

[20] "Something Beautiful" Hymns For The Family of God, Paragon Associates, Inc., Nashville, Tennessee

[21] Phillip Yancey, *The Jesus I Never Knew,* Zondervan Publishing, Grand Rapids, Michigan, 1995, Page 148.

[22] John 13:1–16 Any Translation

[23] Luke 22:1–17; John 13:1–16 Any Translation

[24] John 13:8 NCV

[25] Max Lucado, *A Gentle Thunder,* Word Publishing, Dallas, Texas, 1995, Page 33.

[26] John 13:34 NIV

[27] William T. Joyner, *Ritual In A New Day,* Abingdon Press, Nashville, Tennessee, 1977, Page 29.

[28] Ecclesiastes 4:9–12, NIV

[29] Andrew Hill with John Wooden, *Be Quick but Don't Hurry, Finding Success In The Teachings of a Lifetime;*
Simon and Schuster, New York, New York 10020, 2110 Pages 136–137.

[30] Ibid., Pagd 139

[31] Coach John Wooden, with Steve Jamison, *Wooden,* Contemporary Publishing Company, Lincolnwood, Illinois 60646, 1975, Page 75.

[32] I Corinthians 12:12–27, NCV

[33] Matthew 25:31–46 Any Translation

[34] II Corinthians 6:1 KJV

[35] John 4:1–26 Any Translation

[36] Matthew 19:13–15; Mark 10:13–16; Luke 18:15–17. Any Translation

[37] Luke 23:32–24, Any Translation.

[38] Luke 7:18–23 Any Translation

[39] Matthew 5:16 Any Translation

[40] Luke 6:27–36, Any Translation

[41] Matthew 5:43–47 Any Translation

[42] Matthew 6:5–8 Any Translation

[43] I John 4:13 NIV

[44] James A. Michener, *Sports in America,* Random House, New York, New York, 1976, Page 4.

[45] Tom Chase *B For Berea, The Amazing Story of Berea College Basketball in the Words of the Men Who Played it,*
Volume one. The Overmountain Press, Johnson City, Tennessee, 2000. Page 236.

[46]. Ricky Byrdsong, *Coaching Your Kids In The Game of Life,* Bethany House Publishers, Minneapolis, Minnesota, 2000, Page 130–142.

[47] Charlie Shedd, *Smart Dads I Know,* Sheed and Ward, Inc., New York, New York, 1981,Page 43.

[48] Dan Clark, *Puppies For Sale,* Health Communications, Inc., Deerfield Beach, Florida 1997, Page 7.

[49] I John 3:18 TEV

[50] Psalm 23:6, Msg.

[51] John 14:1–3 Msg.

[52] I Corinthians 2:9 NIV

[53] 2 Corinthians 5:1, TEV

[54] AIS Sports Nutrition, Fueling Your Sport, Basketball, Australian Sports Commission, Internet

[55] WBCA Preferred Trainer Jackie Ansley, WBCA Training Room, "Hydration Is Just The First Step" Internet

[56] Matthew 10:42; Mark 9:41 Any Translation

[57] John 4:1–26. Any Translation

[58] John 4:13 Any Translation

[59] John 19:28 Any Translation

[60] Matthew 23:27 Any Translation

[61] Matthew 16:23 NIV

[62] Luke 1945–46 Any Translation

[63] John 19:29 Any Translation.

[64] Matthew 245:35,40 Any Translation.

[65] Dean Smith *A Coach's Life,* Random House, New York, New York, 1999, pages 144–145.

[66] Harry Sheehy, *Raising A Team Player,* Storey Publishing, North Adams, MA, 2002, Page 23–24

[67] Coach John Wooden with Steve Jamison, *Wooden: A Lifetime of Observations and Reflections On and Off The Court,* Contemporary Books, Chicago, Illinois, 1997, Page 139–141.

[68] Dean Smith, *A Coach's Life,* Random House, New York, New York, 1999, Page 91–92.

[69] Matthew 20:20–27 NIV

[70] Acts 16:7–8 NIV

[71] Romans 8:28 NIV

[72] Genesis 50:20 RSV

[73] Philippians 3:13b-14. Ph

[74] Mitch Albom, *Tuesdays With Morrie,* Doubleday, New York, New York, 1997, portions of pages 118, 119, 120

[75] Tom Chase, *Berea For Berea—The Amazing Story of Berea College Basketball in the Words of the Men Who Played It,* The Overmountain Press, Johnson City, Tennessee, 2000, Pages 289–290

[76] Matthew 6:24–34 Any Translation

[77] Mark Preston, "Doctor Talk," Article on Internet, www.hoophall.com

[78] Walt "Clyde" Frazier, *The Complete Idiot's Guide To*

Basketball, Alpha Books, New York, New York, 1998
Pages 251–252.
[79] 2 Timothy 1:16–18, TEV
[80] John 6:5–13 Any Translation
[81] Author Unknown
[82] Matthew 25:21 Any Translation
[83] Luke 6:12 Any Translation.
[84] Matthew 6:6 Any Translation
[85] Dean Smith, *A Coach's Life,* Random House, Inc., New York, New York, 1999, Page 150.
[86] Fanny J. Crosby, "Rescue the Perishing."
[87] Psalm 40:2 NIV
[88] Luke 10:25–37. Any Translation.
[89] John 3:1–21 Any Translation.
[90] Luke 19:1–10. Any Translation
[91] Ricky Byrdsong, *Coaching Your Kids In The Game Of Life,* Bethany House, Minneapolis, Minnesota, 2000,
Page 78
[92] Mark 9:23 RSV
[93] Matthew 7:7 NIV
[94] 2 Timothy 1:7 NIV
[95] Walt "Clyde Frazier, *The Complete Idiot's Guide To Basketball,* Alpha Books, New York, New York, 1998,
Pages 206–207.
[96] Phil Jackson, *More Than A Game,* Seven Stories Press, New York, New York, 2001, Page 105.
[97] Micah 6:8 NIV
[98] I Corinthians 13:13, NIV
[99] William Barclay, *Daily Celebration,* Word Books, Waco, Texas, 1971, Page 14.
[100] Richard "Digger" Phelps, *Basketball For Dummies* IDG Books Worldwide, Foster City, California, 2000,
Page 195.
[101] Patrick Saunders, article in Denver Post Staff Writer, published Friday, June 4, 2004. Internet
[102] Psalm 34:13, NIV
[103] Proverbs 13:3 TEV
[104] Proverbs 18:7 NIV
[105] James 1:26 NIV
[106] James 3:8–10 TEV

[107] 1 Peter 3:10 NIV

[108] Matthew 12:36–37 NIV

[109] Luke 6:45 NIV

[110] Ephesians 4:29 NIV

[111] Article by Ric Bucher, ESPN Magazine, June 9, 2003, Pages 40–46.

[112] Michael Jordan, *I Can't Accept Not Trying,* Harper, San Francisco, (Found this quote in November 2, 2000 issue of "Bits and Pieces" which is a motivational magazine. Don't know the page number or date of book.)

[113] Philippians 3:13–14. TLB

[114] Mark 14:29 Any Translation

[115] Mark 14:66–72. Any Translation

[116] John 21:15–19. Any Translation

[117] Acts 2:14–41. Any Translation.

[118] Author Unknown, from *Poems That Life Forever,* Hazel Felleman, Editor, Doubleday, 1965

[119] Maxwell Maltz, *Psycho-Cybernetics,* Pocket Books, New York, New York, 1959. Page 123.

[120] Bill Bradley, *Values Of The Game,* Artisan, New York, 1998, Page 79.

[121] Romans 12:1 and 3, NIV

[122] Philippians 2:5–8, NCV

[123] Helmut Thielicke, *Christ And The Meaning Of Life,* Harper and Brothers, New York, New York, 1962, Page 18.

[124] Matthew 26:36–46 Any Translation

[125] Psalm 46:10 NIV

About the Author

Noel White was born in Berea, Kentucky, and spent his early years in Barbourville and Danville, Kentucky. A graduate of Danville High School, he was captain of his basketball team. He graduated from Union College, where he majored in physical education, preparing to become a basketball coach. While working toward a Master's Degree at the University of Tennessee, he felt called to the pastoral ministry. After working for two years as a program director for the Kettering, Ohio, YMCA, he enrolled at Wesley Theological Seminary in Washington DC, where he received a Master of Divinity Degree. He also has a Doctor of Ministry Degree from the Disciples' Seminary, Lexington Theological Seminary in Lexington, Kentucky.

Married to his college sweetheart, Betty Jane, they have two adult children, John Noel and Mary Jane, a daughter-in-law, Lori Kirkland White, and three grandchildren, identical twin grandaughters, Jenna Jewell and Laurel Elizabeth, and grandson, Daniel Noel.

Currently residing in Melrose, Florida, Noel and Betty Jane have served the following ministerial positions:

Nineteen years serving as pastor of United Methodist Churches in Kentucky, fourteen of which were at Trinity Hill United Methodist Church in Lexington, where the membership quadrupled and he was on the radio for ten years.

Eight years serving as pastor in the United Church of Christ, including five years at Shiloh Church in Dayton, Ohio, where the worship services were televised to southwest Ohio, eastern Kentucky; and on VISN, a national network; and two years at Tell City, Indiana.

Twelve years serving as the Chief Executive Office of Penney Retirement Community in Florida, a Christian continuing care facility, during which numerous renovations were completed and new facilities built.

Currently Noel and Betty Jane enjoy serving a small membership Presbyterian Church in San Mateo, Florida, traveling, doing yard work, reading, spending time with their grandchildren and writing for future generations about their family heritage.

TATE PUBLISHING, LLC

127 East Trade Center Terrace
Mustang, Oklahoma 73064

(888) 361 - 9473

TATE PUBLISHING, LLC
www.tatepublishing.com